Daddy, Where Were You?

Healing for the Father-Deprived Daughter

Heather Harpham Kopp

D1603305

SERVANT PUBLICATIONS
ANN ARBOR, MICHIGAN

Vine Books is an imprint of Servant Publications especially designed to serve
evangelical Christians.

Published by Servant Publications
P.O. Box 8617
Ann Arbor, Michigan 48107

Cover design: Paul Higdon
Cover photo: © Superstock. Used by permission.

98 99 00 01 10 9 8 7 6 5 4 3 2 1

Printed in the United States of America
ISBN 1-56955-052-2

LIBRARY OF CONGRESS CATALOGING-IN-PUBLICATION DATA

Kopp, Heather Harpman, 1964-
Daddy, where were you? : healing for the father-deprived daughter / by Heather
Harpman Kopp.
    p.   cm.
Originally published : Lynwood, WA : Aglow Publications, © 1991.
Includes bibliographical references (p.   ).
ISBN 1-56955-052-2 (alk. paper)
1. Fathers and daughters.   2. Parental deprivation.   I. Title.
HQ755.85.K666   1998
306.874'2—dc21
                                                            98-14885
                                                            CIP

CONTENTS

For my sister,
Katherine Hillis Mosby

Introduction

Daddy, Where Were You? was originally published nine years ago. I wrote the book mostly as a means to sort through my own painful father-loss issues. I also hope to help other father-deprived women find healing. But because it was my first book, I worried that it was too personal, too unsophisticated.

I was totally unprepared for the outpouring of letters and calls following its publication. I heard from hundreds of readers, including counselors, pregnancy clinics, and even jail workers. I was especially surprised by how many teenage girls across the country wrote to tell me of the father-shaped void in their hearts. So many wanted to pour out their stories to someone they thought would understand.

During the last few years while *Daddy, Where Were You?* has been out of print, the requests for copies have continued until I have only one dog-eared copy left. I see this as sad proof that the number of daughters encountering disappointment in their relationships with their fathers has not lessened.

When an editor at Servant Publications asked to reissue this book, I was thrilled. I resisted my writerly and egotistical urge to completely rewrite the manuscript, and made few changes aside from updating important personal and factual information.

I continue to see this book as a place for a father-deprived woman to begin a healing process. And I still believe that the best reason to look back at our past for a period of time is so that we can look ahead with more clarity and hope.

I pray that *Daddy, Where Were You?* will help you ask important questions about the impact of your father on key areas of your life: your relationships with men; your sexual identity; and the way you see God. Above all, I pray that it will ultimately lead you onto the lap of your *Abba* Father.

Daddy, Where Were You?

I open a family photo album and see a picture of myself as a small child. Big brown eyes, innocent and happy, gaze out at the world. *Is that really me?* I find it hard to believe I was ever someone's little girl. If it were true, wouldn't I know it? Wouldn't I feel it?

I see pictures of my father, too, on these first few pages. He looks strong, young, and handsome. A few pictures even show him holding me. I must have been his little girl briefly—before divorce made him disappear from my life.

Later, he sent me photos of himself from New York. In the pictures, he stood next to a white car wearing a tan trench coat. With his dark hair and mustache, I thought he looked like Cary Grant. I was so proud and showed the snapshots to all my friends.

"Look, this is my dad!" They thought he was handsome, too.

Years pass as I flip a few more album pages. Suddenly, the pictures of him stop. I am still there, framed in Kodak white, staring out at the camera. But a telltale pout tugs at the corners of my mouth.

Daddy, where were you?

The Father-Shaped Void

Where was your daddy when you were a little girl?

Was he walking down shaded streets next to you, leaning over a bit so he could hold your hand? Was he seemingly everywhere—in the kitchen busy with Mom, outside playing with your brothers—but always available for you, his daughter? Did he read bedtime stories to you at night and whisper silly secrets in your ear?

Or do you have splintered memories of your father? Was his hand too high to reach, his pace too fast to match? Did he come home drunk at night, hours after you'd gone to bed, and never kiss your sleeping face?

Did he bruise your skin or defile you? Do you have no memory of him at all?

Few of us can claim the first scenario—the loving, adoring daddy. Too many of us relate to unhappier versions of life with Dad. One day we looked up and Daddy wasn't available. We'd lost him, or at least the part of him we needed.

That was yesterday. Today we are grown women, some of us with husbands and children of our own. On the surface, it appears we are no longer affected by the father-loss we experienced as children. But in our hearts is a father-shaped void. Somewhere inside, a little girl still searches for all her father failed to give her.

Where Have All the Fathers Gone?

Father-absence, probably the most prevalent form of father-loss, is growing. From 1930 to 1990, the number of children living without a father in the home doubled from 17 percent to 36 percent. Today, the figure continues to rise; some estimate it will rise to 60 percent in the nineties.[1]

These figures don't take into account the millions more families in which a father is physically present but not involved with his children in meaningful ways.

The good news is that today many men are trying to reverse this trend. Awareness of how father-absence negatively affects not only individual children but society as a whole is growing. But clearly, the battle ahead looms large.

So where have all the fathers gone?

The explosion of divorce in the last half-century is the greatest single factor behind the disappearance of Dad. As millions of marriages dissolved, millions of children lost their fathers. Daddy became a visiting stranger—or, worse yet, vanished altogether.

Death, of course, is another common cause of father-loss. A photo, a tombstone, and a blurred memory are all that remain to remind some daughters they once had a father. They can't escape the feeling of abandonment.

Millions more women grew up in homes where the father was physically present, but for varying reasons failed to provide the love, support, and attention his daughter needed. Alcoholism and drug dependency may have destroyed Dad's ability to effectively parent. Unpredictable and unstable, Daddy was a man to be loved and feared, but never counted on.

Still other women grew up with workaholic fathers. Their dads succeeded in business or career to the detriment of their families. Try though they might, these daughters could not crack their father's world. They could only stand outside knocking, waiting and hoping that someday he wouldn't be so busy.

Many women "lost" their fathers through physical, emotional, or sexual abuse.

The reasons for father-loss could go on: physical sickness, mental illness, incarceration, and so on. In this book, I define the victim of "father-loss" broadly enough to include any daughter whose father was absent, ineffective, neglectful, distant, abusive—in short, any daughter who, although she had a father, never had a "daddy."

Many of our fathers fall into more than one of the above categories. Usually, the more that apply, the greater the consequences of father-loss upon our lives. These consequences, however, are not always obvious.

Do You Need This Book?

Regina McGlothin, M.D, is a practicing psychiatrist in Eugene, Oregon. She agrees that while father-loss is widespread, often women don't recognize how it continues to affect them as adults. She counsels many women with problems that on the surface appear unrelated to their fathers. "But sooner or later," she says, "we end up talking about Dad."[2]

Our fathers were the first men we ever loved. If they were absent or ineffective, our views of ourselves, men, and God are greatly influenced. How would you answer the following questions?

1. Do you now, or have you in the past, compromised yourself to gain the approval or acceptance of a man?

2. Is it hard for you to trust men?

3. Are you uncomfortable around men, often avoiding eye contact?

4. Do you suffer from nebulous feelings of worthlessness that are hard to trace?

5. Do you feel the need for a strong father-figure in your life?

6. Do you see yourself as you think your father saw you (i.e., abandonable, unimportant, stupid)?

7. Are you unable to fully forgive your father for his absence, neglect, or abuse?

8. Is your present relationship (or lack thereof) with your father still painful today?

9. Do you have difficulty trusting God?

10. Is it hard for you to identify with God as Father?

If you answered yes to even one of these questions, you could benefit from reading this book. Not because I have any magic formulas or speedy remedies, but because we share a God who longs to bring redemption to our lives.

Let Nothing Be Wasted

Why discuss what has happened in the past? Isn't today what's important?

Today and tomorrow are what count. Unfortunately, the past rarely stays where it belongs. It has a way of blowing debris and branches from behind us onto the road in front of us. When we stumble over these remnants, the past is no longer just the past. It has become part of our present and needs to be addressed.

Remember the familiar Bible story where Jesus miraculously fed five thousand people with five fish and two barley loaves? Afterward, when everyone had eaten their fill, he said to his disciples, "Gather the pieces that are left over. Let nothing be wasted" (Jn 6:12).

This Scripture doesn't apply only to our three-year-old son who won't eat his peas. Jesus is more concerned about our lives than he is about food. He doesn't want to waste *anything*, including our pain from the past.

The rejection and disappointment of father-loss crushed us inside. But Jesus wants to redeem the broken pieces of our hearts. He can salvage and use what we want to bury and hide. He alone can gather together the crumbs that have fallen from our childhoods and see that they help, rather than hurt, our futures.

"'For I know the plans I have for you,' declares the Lord, 'plans to prosper you and not to harm you, plans to give you hope and a future'" (Jer 29:11).

Not only can God redeem the past, he can ensure that our search for a father doesn't end in disappointment and disillusionment—or, as you will read in Sharon's case, in tragedy.

Sharon

I have encountered scores of hurting daughters. But one of the most wrenching accounts of father-loss is contained in Marilee P. Dunker's book *Days of Glory, Seasons of Night.*

Dunker's now-deceased father, Bob Pierce, was a renowned evangelist in the 1950s and founded World Vision. Her book chronicles her father's great faith and commitment to spreading the gospel in foreign countries. But she is also painfully honest about the family he left behind as he traveled the world doing God's work.

"Although we knew he loved us," she writes, "he was gone too much to be involved with our everyday lives, and it was impossible to fill him in on a month's worth of life during two dinners and a trip to Disneyland."

Dunker and her younger sister never knew what it was to have their dad at home. However, Dunker's older sister, Sharon, did. Sharon was eight years old when their father started traveling. "Only God knows the damage that was done when suddenly she [Sharon] lost her daddy to a work that demanded all his thoughts, energy and time," writes Dunker.

During her twenties, Sharon developed emotional problems and fell into deep depression. "Her overwhelming need for love and approval from the men in her life and her need to feel useful and significant drove Sharon deeper and deeper into the pit of despair. Her whole life had been spent like that little girl of long ago, earnestly waving her hand with a desperate desire to be acknowledged, but somehow always being overlooked in the crowd."

After a suicide attempt and a stay in a sanitarium, Dunker's sister began to pick up the pieces of her life. But then a devastating end to a romance shoved her over the edge. At age twenty-seven, Sharon committed suicide.[3]

Dunker's story moved me in part because my own sister attempted suicide, but even more because it vividly portrays the pain, tragedy, and searching that so often accompany father-loss.

The Legacy of Father-Loss

Of course, most women who suffer from father-loss will not take their own lives, and the father-daughter relationship alone isn't directly responsible for Sharon's choice. So many other factors play a part in our adult choices. And each of us responds differently to our father-loss. Factors such as our age at the time, our mother's reaction, and the availability of male role models all play a part in determining how father-loss influences our lives.

And yet, it is still helpful to discuss certain problems associated with a painful father experience that seem fairly universal. They are the "heart issues" that comprise the legacy of father-loss. Dunker's sister, Sharon, demonstrated several of these: despair, low self-esteem, and intense longing for male approval and acceptance.

The following chapters are devoted to identifying and dealing with these and other issues. Here is a quick preview of issues to be covered:

Sexual identity. If indeed Daddy was the first man we ever loved and then he rejected us, we may feel as if we've failed as females. We may have never developed confidence in our own femininity and lovableness. We'll discuss how this eventually affects the way we interact sexually with men and why so many father-deprived daughters fall into promiscuity.

Relationships with men. We'll explore how father-loss influences the way we feel toward men. Do we have difficulty trusting men? Are we afraid of them? Do we glorify them, expecting perfection? Do we try to get other men to give us what our fathers didn't? Do we transfer onto our husbands expectations and resentments rooted in feelings toward our fathers?

Self-esteem. We'll examine ways our father-loss may have directly or inadvertently damaged our self-concepts. What coping strategies do we use to deal with our feelings of low self-worth? How can we develop true self-esteem based on our identity as God's daughters?

Ideas about God. Do we have a correct image of God, or is it warped because of negative experiences with our fathers? Do we have difficulty believing that our heavenly Father won't let us down, as our earthly father did? How can we experience God's Father-love?

I hope this book will help you discover which of these issues apply to you. Beyond that, I hope to give you an opportunity to grieve the loss of your father if you haven't yet; to get angry at him if you need to; to come to a place where you can forgive him. You may want to keep a journal while you read. Often, as we write about our feelings, we better understand ourselves as well as what it is God might be trying to say to us.

Above all, I want to share with you a journey that will hurt at times but will ultimately lead to a place of healing and a relationship with God you might not have imagined possible.

Psalm 27:10 reads, "Though my father and mother forsake me, the Lord will receive me." God alone can turn our father-loss into gain. Will you let him?

Time to Consider

Isaiah prophesied of Jesus who later spoke these words, "The Spirit of the Sovereign Lord is on me, because the Lord has anointed me to preach good news to the poor. He has sent me to bind up the brokenhearted, to proclaim freedom for the captives and release from darkness for the prisoners" (Is 61:1).

1. How does this Scripture apply to your father-loss? In what way are you brokenhearted? Do you sense you are still blind to some of the consequences of father-loss on your life? In what areas do you need to be set free?

2. Where was your father when you were a little girl? Where do you feel God was?

3. What emotions do you experience most when you think of your father? Pain? Anger? Apathy? A feeling of deadness? Why?

4. Read Ephesians 6:4 and 1 Thessalonians 2:11, 12. What does God expect of a father?

5. How do you feel your dad failed to fulfill God's plan for fathers?

I'll Do Anything

*F*rom the time I was two until my parents divorced when I was six, my father was addicted to amphetamines. He developed a drug-related psychosis as a result, and his behavior often bordered on the bizarre and abusive. Of the few incidents I can recall from this period, one involved a train trip that never took place—except where it counted most, in my heart.

"Heather, you and Jimmy pack your clothes now," Dad said one day. "We're going on a train trip."

My four-year-old brother jumped up and down. "Heather, hurry up. We're going on a train!" I wanted to be excited, too. A train trip sounded thrilling. So why was I so worried? My mother sat at the dining room table paying bills. I tapped her arm. "Are we going on a train?"

"No," she said firmly. "No one is going anywhere."

My dad ignored her words. "Sure we are!" he insisted. "You and Jimmy and I are going on a train, Heather. Won't that be fun?"

I stood silently.

"Now get ready. Get your coat!" he demanded.

Still I hesitated. I adored my dad and couldn't bear the

thought of him leaving on a train without me. But an unknown fear squeezed my chest.

I ran to the other side of my mother's chair. My father chased me, and for several moments we maneuvered around the table.

Finally, in frustration, my dad grabbed Jimmy and dashed out the door. Mom raced after him. Moments later, she flew back into the house to phone the police. Her face was red and tear-stained. "He's got Jimmy!" she yelled at no one in particular.

Police pursued my father's car at high speeds. When they finally caught him, they returned Jimmy to my mother and admitted my dad to a mental hospital, where he spent the next two months.

I don't remember where my mother told me my dad had gone. I assumed he'd left on the train without me.

I did the right thing in refusing to go with my father that day. He was at the height of his illness, and it would have been dangerous to cooperate with him. Besides, he never made it to the train.

My adult mind knows this. Nevertheless, the little-girl part of me has always regretted my decision. It's as if in that single moment, I lost my father. I let my daddy get away. I missed the train.

What's in a Daddy?

Have you ever prepared a recipe without a key ingredient? It didn't taste quite right. You knew something was missing, but you couldn't put your finger on it until you reread the recipe. "Aha!" you declared. "No wonder my cookies were so bland. I forgot the nutmeg."

In the same way, to understand the consequences of father-loss in your life, you need to know what it was you missed. What are daddies made of? What crucial ingredients do they add to the lives of their little girls?

One important role of a father is to help his daughter develop a positive sexual identity. He largely determines how she feels about her femaleness and how she sees herself in relationship to the opposite sex.

One way he does this is to encourage her to adopt feminine qualities. Elyce Wakerman writes in *Father-Loss*, "While mother may provide the model of femininity, it is father who motivates daughter to imitate feminine behavior."[1]

We watched Mommy apply makeup, spray perfume, and fix her hair. She was our role model, and it was her clothes closet we raided when we wanted to play dress-up. But it was the light that shone (or didn't shine) in Daddy's eyes when we wore our frilly pink Easter dresses that made us glad to be little girls.

A father's contribution to his daughter's sexual identity goes beyond affirming her femininity. He also models her first inter-action with the opposite sex and greatly influences her future relationships with men. If Daddy loves his little girl, she will more easily believe that another man could someday. If Daddy gives her physical warmth and affection, she will be less likely to search for that affection through empty, misguided, or promiscuous relationships with men.

A father's role is especially vital during certain stages of childhood. For example, children between the ages of three and six may "fall in love" with the parent of the opposite sex. For example, a four-year-old son in this stage might be more affectionate and attentive than usual to his mother, and perhaps even announce that when he grows up, he wants to marry her!

This stage is not only normal, it is an important part of a child's development.

Imagine for a moment the impact on a daughter who is in this stage—in love with her brave, strong daddy—and suddenly he disappears. What if he is too busy, too ill, or too hungover to notice her need for his affection? What if rather than hugging and loving his little girl, he berates or abuses her? What if he isn't around for his daughter to "fall in love" with in the first place? What happens when Daddy, a major influence on a woman's positive sexual identity, is absent from her life as a little girl?

My brothers used to dig out "magic invisible pens" from the cereal boxes. They'd work for at least a day. The boys would write a message with special invisible ink, and only when they held it under a light did the marks made earlier appear.

The wounds to the sexual identity of the father-deprived daughter are often invisible during her early years. Not until the agonies of adolescence descend—the awkwardness over the development of her body, the heartaches of puppy love—do her wounds begin to show.

Boys Here, Boys There, Boys, Boys, Everywhere!

I looked for the one my heart loves; I looked for him but did not find him.

SONG OF SOLOMON 3:1

I was twelve years old and Joey was the first love of my life. Actually, we hardly spoke a word to each other. Not that it mattered. He was my god—gorgeous, popular, and alas, unattainable. I spent two years mooning over him from afar.

The first two years of high school I spent similarly infatuated. This time a hunky, blue-eyed, much-sought-after guy broke my heart. Yet again, I didn't speak more than twenty words to him the entire time of my lovesickness. Years later I realized I had only adored his glorified image, his unreachableness.

Many psychiatrists would agree that through these infatuations, I relived the rejection I felt from my dad. In doing so, I attempted to mourn the loss of my father. This makes sense to me. By choosing someone I knew I couldn't have, I spared myself the possibility of an actual repeat rejection.

When, at seventeen, I fell in love with my husband-to-be and he with me, it was an obsessive, terrifying feeling. Unrequited love had finally been answered, but a train trip from the past reminded me that those who love me might leave me. I'd let my daddy get away. This time would be different. I'd do anything.

"Anything" resulted in pregnancy. Tom and I married during Christmas vacation of our senior year in high school.

And unfortunately, we divorced shortly after our ten-year high school reunion. Even though I had begun working on and writing about my own father-issues while we were still married, those issues were only one aspect of the problems Tom and I shared.

If you lost your father, you too probably entered adolescence desperate for male attention. One day you looked up from your desk at school, and in a boy's smile you recognized hope. Here was a male, like your father. Maybe...

In the seventies, Dr. E. Mavis Hetherington conducted one of the first major studies of father-absent adolescent girls. The results of her studies are still commonly cited today and have been confirmed by other studies.

Hetherington found that these daughters had a harder time relating comfortably and appropriately with males than did the group of father-present girls. How the girls handled their feelings of awkwardness, however, tended to vary according to the type of loss.

The daughters of divorce, for example, usually chose the seat closest to the male interviewer. They talked easily; assumed a sprawled, relaxed posture; and were anxious for attention. These girls became sexually active early and often behaved promiscuously. They were likely to have a negative view of their father and of men in general.

The daughters whose fathers had died were reserved, perhaps because their loss was so final. They chose the chair farthest away from the male interviewer, spoke little, and made little eye contact. Their dating patterns were delayed as they often maintained a glorified image of their deceased fathers, an image no other male could measure up to.[2]

Hetherington's findings suggest that the way we lost our fathers affects the way we view and respond to males. However, behaviors associated with various types of father-loss do not always fit into rigid categories.

Think back to your adolescence. What did boys mean to you? And how did your father-loss influence your response to them?

Some of you found that your awkwardness with these strange male creatures was stronger than your need for their attention. You swallowed your desire and stood back out of fear of rejection.

Others of you looked to the "love" of a boy as the key to your happiness. Your heart cried out, I'll do anything—even to the point of promiscuity.

Promiscuity: An Empty Promise

I opened for my lover, but my lover had left; he was gone. My heart sank at his departure. I looked for him but did not find him. I called him but he did not answer.

SONG OF SOLOMON 5:6

Promiscuity is a widely acknowledged consequence of father-deprivation. In *Fatherless America*, David Blankenhorn Jr. explains, "Many studies confirm that girls who grow up without fathers are at much greater risk for early sexual activity, adolescent childbearing, divorce."[3]

Were you promiscuous in the past? If so, this appetite for affection probably began to gnaw away inside you sometime in adolescence. You heard a voice that whispered promises of love. You played hard to get only for a moment, if at all. You made rash, foolish choices; your need for affection overshadowed the risks involved.

Usually, the boy abandoned you. The love you sought was still out of reach. You went back for more. Logic failed. You'd do anything....

Diane is a pastor's wife, a devoted stay-at-home mother of two young children. Her life today, however, is hardly a reflection of her past.

Diane's mother and father divorced when she was ten. "My father committed adultery, and that's what split them up," she says. "Afterwards, when my mother got pregnant out of wedlock, all of my morals and values went out the window."

Both of Diane's parents remarried quickly. "But my stepfather was mean to me, so I went to live with my dad when I was fourteen," she explains. "He didn't have any rules or care what I did. I was free there, but my home was empty, and I turned to friends and boys for fulfillment."

Diane experimented with sexual foreplay at age thirteen and had her first intercourse at fifteen. "I was on LSD at the time. I didn't even like the boy, but I thought this meant he liked me. It meant acceptance, being cool."

By the time Diane was a senior in high school, she was having sex with "whomever I wanted." "My dad," she says, her voice shaky with emotion, "knew what was going on but didn't even care if I came home at night. He said, 'Diane, you better get on birth control.' On the inside, I was pleading with him to tell me that he loved me, that he didn't want to see me hurt or used. He never did."

After Diane graduated from high school, she obtained fake identification and entered the bar scene. "I would sleep with two or three different men a week," she says. "I don't even remember the names of most of those guys."

Diane's past echoes that of millions of women. Her experience also demonstrates that it isn't just a lack of affection from Dad that contributes to the sexual choices we make growing up.

If your father was absent or ineffective, you were missing more than just hugs. Your sexual identity and your tendency toward promiscuity (if it applies) may also have been influenced by:

Lack of moral training. If your father was absent or unavailable, Mom was busy trying to cope. Maybe no one took the time to teach you about morality. Perhaps your own mother or father had sleep-over dates. Sex outside of marriage was never presented as sin. With no guidelines or values, promiscuous behavior seemed natural to you.

Unguarded chastity. Daddy is the one who traditionally stands guard over his daughter's virginity. He emphasizes chastity and purity. If no one guarded your virginity, chances are you felt it was of little value, and you might have quickly discarded it.

Low self-esteem. Due in part to father-loss, you may have grown up convinced you weren't lovable, special, or important. So you grabbed what little love you could get, even if that meant compromise. You feared the moment when a guy would recognize your worthlessness. Besides, you hardly felt good enough about yourself to actually reject someone else.

Doubts about femininity. As noted earlier, Daddy determines our confidence in our femininity. Author David Popenoe writes, "They [girls] learn to appreciate their own femininity from the one male who is most special in their lives. Most importantly, through loving and being loved by their father, they learn that they are love-worthy."[4]

How love-worthy did your father make you feel? Without a father to give you confidence in your femininity and dawning womanhood, you may have felt you had something to prove.

Confusion. When an adolescent begins to mature, often her relationship with her father drastically changes. "Ironically," notes one Purdue researcher, "just as a teenage girl is entering adolescence and going through the outward and often awkward change that goes along with puberty, her father pulls away from her because he isn't comfortable with his daughter's new sexuality. So just at the point when she needs approving hugs from him the most, he's less likely to give them to her."[5]

If your father was around, how did he respond to you as you matured? Did he still hug you? Too much? Or did he treat you with a "hands off" policy?

The Search Continues

During adolescence, our childhood wounds began to throb, insecurities gulped us down whole, and our quest for love became an obsession. We moved into adulthood still desperately searching for Daddy.

Eventually, most of us married. According to the study Wakerman conducted for *Father-Loss*, the father-absent daughter is more likely than the two-parent daughter to seek marriage. To her, marriage represents normalcy, security, and a chance to reclaim what was lost. Unfortunately, she is also more likely to report "significant problems" in her marriage and to divorce or separate.[6]

One possible reason for this is her choice of mate. The daughter of an absent or troubled father often marries a husband with similar traits—and one who is ill-equipped to handle the emotional needs and demands of a father-deprived wife.

The daughter whose father died has a unique problem. Often, she may marry a man who seems to fit the bill of a perfect "daddy" but who can never hope to measure up to her idealized image of her deceased father.

The daughter of divorce often establishes a pattern of loss and broken relationships. She tends to repeat, as if compelled by an invisible force, the pattern of pain and estrangement. When my first husband and I divorced, we were further devastated to realize that we were both about the same age our parents had been when they divorced, and that our own kids were close to our own ages at that time.

A second reason the father-deprived daughter encounters

troubled waters in marriage is that she expects it will heal her wounds. Instead, it inflames them. She may have found love, but the question remains: Can she believe in it? Old insecurities and resentments buried in childhood rise up to find vent in her new home. She gazes into the eyes of her husband only to find herself face to face with the unmet "father-needs" of her childhood.

Time to Consider

1. How did your father build or crush your femininity?

2. If you were promiscuous in the past, how do you feel about sex today?

3. How do you think God responds to sexual sin? Is sexual sin harder for him to forgive than other types of sin? Why or why not? Read John 8:1-11.

4. If you were promiscuous in the past, how do you feel today toward the men with whom you had sex? Have you forgiven them? Have you asked God to forgive you? Have you forgiven yourself?

5. How are you saying "I'll do anything" in yet a different way today? Describe any areas of your life where you still compromise yourself in order to feel loved.

6. Do you see yourself as a whole and complete person outside of a relationship with a man? Why or why not?

t h r e e

Won't You Be My Daddy?

*A*bout a year after the train incident with my dad, I got a chance to go on a real train. But this time I was forced to leave him behind.

Despite his two-month stay at a mental hospital, my father's drug and mental problems had escalated. My mother pleaded with him to get help, but he refused. Urged by friends and relatives, she finally gave him an ultimatum: Either he would enter and complete a drug-rehabilitation program, or she would divorce him. Meanwhile, she would take us kids to live with her mother in Washington.

Friends of the family drove us to the train station in New Jersey. When I asked my mom why Daddy wasn't coming, she reassured me, "Daddy is going to a special school. He'll get well soon, and we'll all be back together again."

Oblivious to the hard facts behind her words, I never dreamed that I would not see my father again for many years. And I never dreamed how great a void the lack of him, mentally ill or not, would leave in my heart.

Daughter for Hire

The other day I drove past a thinly clad, dusty-looking man sitting on the corner of a busy intersection. He held a sign that read: "Will work for food." You've probably seen others like him with similar signs. Each time, I'm taken aback by such bold declarations of neediness.

We saw in the previous chapter how father-loss sent us in search of physical affection from men. But we grew up desperate to fulfill another kind of need as well. Our hunger was less advertised, but if our hearts had worn signs, they might have read: *Daughter for hire! Will love, adore, and idolize father-figure in return for parental guidance, advice, and approval.*

Remember Sharon from chapter one who eventually took her life? She once wrote: "I know Mom loves me. But some things a woman just can't give—one being the comfort of a man, yes, a father even, when he puts his arms around you and says everything will be OK"[1]

There is something unique about a loving father's authority, strength, and leadership. We went in search of that "something" as little girls. You may remember looking to an older brother, uncle, or teacher as a father-figure. *Care about me!* you silently pleaded. *Put your arm around me and talk to me as if I matter.*

Perhaps your cry was answered. The thrill of your school years was in seventh grade when you were a male teacher's "class pet." Or perhaps your grandfather took you under his aged but tender arm.

Yet, just as the man with the sign isn't always offered food or work, the father-deprived daughter isn't always offered the fathering she seeks.

So Close and Yet So Far

When my children were small, they rarely thought to ask for toys. They could live without the latest remote-control-flying-combat-monster, unless they saw it. A trip to the toy store was guaranteed to evoke the most pitiful begging the world ever witnessed.

Similarly, we who grew up not knowing a father's love were often unaware of what we were missing. But to see a "father" we wanted but couldn't have was almost more than we could take.

Shelly's dad abandoned her family when she was two. She doesn't remember him, but her mother told her that he was a musician who made his living as a professional piano player. When I asked Shelly how she'd felt about men growing up, she related the following story.

"We had this neat music teacher in junior high school," she said. "Everyone liked him a lot, including me, but I acted the opposite. I was a cooperative straight-A student in all my other classes, but I was sarcastic and disruptive in his.

"As a matter of fact," she continued, "I did the same thing in high school. The music teacher was a nice man; in fact, now he's the pastor of my church! But back then ... I can't believe how terribly I treated him."

Shelly's music teachers reminded her of her absent father.

This attracted her to them. But she became angry when she realized she was only one of many students instead of being somehow special. Through these teachers, Shelly experienced the rejection of her father. And through her anger at them, she punished the daddy that never was—as well as these potential surrogates who were oblivious to her need.

The Adult in Search of Daddy

Imagine our world if adults behaved like children: Grown men at their jobs would break into fits of tears because they forgot their lunch boxes. Women in grocery stores would pull out each other's hair in a squabble over who reached the checkout aisle first. (Granted, that actually happens from time to time.) No one would walk anywhere—everyone would run or skip from place to place just for the fun of it.

These pictures are ridiculous. Yet inside each of us lives a small child, a part of our personality that never quite grew up. Because our "father-needs" weren't met in childhood, our "little girl" exerts herself in our adult life in an effort to get these needs met. Thus, we keep the search for a daddy alive long after we may think we've abandoned it.

According to Dr. McGlothlin, this childlike search for a father-figure makes women vulnerable. "They need a strong, almighty figure," she explains, "who is powerful and whom they can adopt as father."[2]

A common scenario is the woman who attempts to gain the acceptance and attention of a friend's father, her pastor, or perhaps an uncle. She becomes frustrated and disappointed if these men don't provide the fathering she seeks.

Once, some years back, a middle-aged relative of mine named Mark arrived in town for a visit. He happened to look quite a bit like my father. And although he had this stern, strong personality, I'd always liked him and wanted him to like me.

I greeted Mark at the door with a joking barb. He laughed and returned one of his own. I felt accepted. As the night wore on, however, he became quiet. Too quiet. Immediately I feared the worst. "I've always known he doesn't like me," I told my husband.

The next day the three of us had to travel two hours in the car together. Mark drove. We'd driven in near silence about ten minutes when he reached up and adjusted the rearview mirror so he could see me in the back seat. "Well, Heather," he said sternly, "I think we'd better talk."

Suddenly I felt like a twelve-year-old. My face flushed, and panic began to claw at my heart.

"I almost turned right around and drove back to Wyoming last night," he said. "I didn't come here to be treated like you've treated me."

I was almost too shocked to answer. "What did I do?" I asked, my voice shaking.

"I didn't appreciate all your smart remarks last night," he answered. "This has gone on for some time. You've got some problem with me, and we're going to solve it right now."

What was he saying? His words were like a terrible hurting dream—the kind you want to run from but can't.

I haltingly tried to explain that the last thing I wanted to do was make him angry. That was my biggest fear. "The remarks were only jokes, icebreakers," I said. "I thought it was safe to do that. I thought we liked each other and ..." I'd tried not to cry, but tears slipped stubbornly down my face.

He listened, brows furrowed, to my pleas of innocence. I think he understood, but he still insisted that I held animosity toward him.

I looked at my husband, but obviously he wasn't about to interfere.

"If anything," I finally admitted, "sometimes I just wish I was ..." a lump the size of a lemon formed in my throat. "Well, more like your daughter or something."

There, I'd said it.

"But you don't act that way!" he answered.

"I'm afraid for you to know how I feel," I said.

He adjusted the mirror again and stared at me so intently I worried he'd drive off the road. "Heather, I love you as if you were my own daughter. Do you understand?"

I looked away and wiped my wet eyes. "All right," I said. "I understand."

For hours after that conversation my gut ached. But I learned something that day. I'd wanted Mark to be a father to me, but my neediness made me afraid to let him come close. In fact, it made me push him away for fear of rejection.

The conflict with my relative gave me valuable insight into myself. But such is not always the case. Often a woman feels a need and pursues a certain response from a man, never realizing she is trying to fill her "father-void." Only as she comes to understand her suppressed longing for a father-figure can she hope to sort through her feelings in the relationship.

Of course, the father-deprived daughter doesn't only look for Daddy in a father-in-law, pastor, or friend. If she marries, she looks to her husband. In the bonds of matrimony, her search continues.

Looking for Daddy in Hubby

If before marriage our "little girl" inside struggled to find voice in our lives, after marriage, her efforts may double.

Ephesians 5:31 reads: "For this reason a man [or woman] *will leave his father and mother* and be united to his wife [or husband], and the two will become one flesh" (italics added).

This Scripture often presents a problem to the father-deprived daughter. To *leave* her father is difficult when she never really had him. She enters marriage still trying to get her father-needs met.

You've probably never said to your husband, "Won't you be my daddy?" But through your words, attitudes, and actions, you may have asked him to do just that.

Josh McDowell once wrote, "A common marital problem is that of a woman relating emotionally to her husband as if he were her father.... Such women often have marital and sexual problems that they don't understand or don't seem able to control."[3]

The father-deprived daughter subconsciously expects her husband to be what her father wasn't. But at the same time, she places on him resentments rooted in her relationship (or lack thereof) with her father. Her husband is expected to fill a chasm he doesn't realize exists. Meanwhile, he bears the brunt of hostility that the wife really feels toward her father.

My first husband, Tom, often found himself in such a position. I wanted him to be the dad I never had—strong, caring, protective. But the minute he tried to be those things, I found myself feeling rebellious and angry. "Who are you to tell me anything! You don't really love me...."

Psychologists refer to such displaced feelings as "transference," which is usually evidenced by a person overreacting to a situation. Trust, submission, and sex are among the favorite trading posts of these displaced emotions.

Trust

The father-deprived daughter often finds herself in a tug-of-war. One moment she clings to a man and cries out; "I'll do anything," and the next she pulls back: "But I don't believe you'll stay."

The most commonly transferred emotion the father-deprived daughter deals with is distrust. Ultimately, she believes that any man she trusts will hurt or abandon her as her father did.

Jean, for example, says her husband can't reassure her enough that he loves her. "I drive him crazy asking him, 'Do you love me?'" Jean's dad never told her that he loved her, and then he died when she was twelve years old.

Feelings of distrust may also lead to feelings of discomfort around men in general. Many women are uncomfortable making eye contact with men other than their husbands. Other women, whose fathers withheld any kind of affirmation, find it difficult to receive admiration or compliments from men.

Submission

It's understandable that a woman with an abusive or domineering father would experience hostile feelings toward men in authority. Some father-deprived daughters find it difficult to allow any man to have control over them. Unloving, ineffective, and authoritarian fathers have added fuel to the fire of the feminist movement.

The issue of submission, of course, has the greatest implications in marriage. Ephesians 5:22-23 says, "Wives, submit to your husbands as to the Lord. For the husband is the head of the wife as Christ is the head of the church, his body, of which he is the Savior." Husbands are in turn admonished, "Love your wives, just as Christ loved the church" (Eph 5:25).

The picture here is of a capable wife, equal in standing with her husband, willingly surrendering to him the final say in matters that concern them.

But as Dr. James Dobson points out, "A woman's willingness to accept the loving leadership of her husband is significantly influenced by the way she perceived the authority of her father. If her father was overbearing, uncaring or capricious during her developmental years, she may attempt to grab the reins of leadership from her future husband."[4]

Linda's alcoholic father failed to provide financially for their family while she grew up. Today, her husband is between jobs and unemployed.

"I wanted this new dress at the mall the other day, but he said we couldn't afford it," she says. "My anger toward him was extreme, even though I knew he couldn't help it. I went back later and bought the dress anyway."

Like Linda, you may have grown up a victim of circumstances out of your control. Your family collapsed around you like a flimsy house of cards, blown apart by your dad's absence or neglect. Have you transferred resentment toward your father to your husband? This time, do you want to be the one in control of placing the important cards?

Often we cloak our need to control. Maybe you don't outwardly rebel against your husband as Linda did, but do you manipulate him to get your own way?

Sexual Responsiveness

A tendency toward promiscuity often characterizes the sexual behavior of father-deprived daughters prior to marriage. But after marriage these same women find themselves turned off to sex, even repulsed by it.

Kate, twenty-eight, married Syd, forty-two. She says, "I was looking for a strong, fatherly husband. I got one. But now I can't stand for him to touch me. Our marriage is OK. I feel secure with Syd, but our sex life is almost nonexistent."

Kate feels repulsed by Syd because emotionally she relates to him as a father. McDowell puts it this way: "Not having had their needs met for non-erotic, fatherly affection, they [father-deprived daughters] may unconsciously be responding to their mate's physical affection as they would should affection from their fathers turn to sexual foreplay."[5]

Even women who don't marry daddy-types may transfer father-directed hostility to their husbands. After years of not receiving affection from their fathers, they find it hard to accept what they conclude must be insincere, phony, or undeserved affection now.

Understanding the Search

Is it *always* wrong to relate to your husband or another man in a fatherly way? No. Sometimes a man can meet an unmet father-need in a healthy way. But rarely does that happen until we have sorted out our feelings and motives, and understand what we really want—and what we should expect and ask for.

Problems arise, though, when we grasp for a certain response and resent our husbands when we don't get it. Let's face it. Most men don't want to be our daddies. And they don't know how to decipher the frantic "father-wanted" signs that our inner child has scrawled across our hearts.

What's a woman in need of a father-figure to do? In a future chapter we'll talk about how we can find the father we need in God. Meanwhile, it helps to understand the dynamics behind our search.

Ask yourself:

What did I need from my father that I didn't get? Make a list. These unmet needs have most likely become transferred expectations.

What did my father do that I resented (if he was even present at all)? Make a second list. Note especially the things your dad did that you continue to resent him for today.

Now, consider your relationship with your husband—or someone who might be a potential father-figure in your life. What are repeated points of conflict or hurt? Look over your lists. Can you make any connections? Are you transferring expectations or resentments to your husband or another man?

Understanding our search for a father is a process. So is change. Be patient with yourself. A month from now you may have an argument with your husband and suddenly a light will click on: *I think part of my anger or hurt here is truly directed at my father.*

As you come to understand your search for a father-figure, you will come to better understand yourself—including that little girl inside who is still asking, *Daddy, where were you?*

Time to Consider

1. Pick one word that best describes the little girl part of you. Is she fearful? Insecure? Angry? Vulnerable? Why?

2. In your childhood, who acted as a surrogate father? Or, who did you want to adopt as a father-figure but received no response? How did this make you feel?

3. Review your lists. Which do you have more of—unmet father-needs or father-directed resentments? Why?

4. In what ways are you still searching for a father-figure?

5. Imagine you do have an intelligent, respectable, loving father. He sends you flowers on your birthday. He calls often, wanting to know the latest goings-on in your life. No matter what you tell him, he is on your side. He sometimes offers fatherly advice. Before he hangs up the phone, he always says, "I love you bunches, honey." Would having such a father change who you are? How?

f o u r

Mother ... and the "Other"

*M*y father never completed his drug program. He dropped out of treatment a few weeks after we left on the train. Six months later he reenrolled, but it was too late. My mother had met another man in Washington. She married him within days of her divorce from my dad.

At first, my mother's remarriage meant little more to me than Pop-Tarts and chocolate milk, luxuries we couldn't afford on welfare. But as time passed, I grew resentful of this "other man." Rather than filling my father-void, my stepfather only cemented it more firmly into place.

I immediately drew up a plan of attack against my stepfather. I was sarcastic, loud, hostile. Not surprisingly, he responded in kind. Angry words, slammed doors, and violent outbursts became a daily part of family life.

The conflicts with my stepdad worsened as I neared adolescence. I was twelve years old when one night during an especially hot argument, I pulled a butcher knife out of the kitchen drawer. "I hate you so much!" I screamed, waving my weapon. "You are not my father, and don't you ever forget it!"

I never used the knife, but the incident prompted my

mother to take me to a child psychiatrist. I was rude and unco-operative with the doctor. Toward the end of my session, he said, "Heather, I'd really like to see you again."

"At forty bucks a shot," I answered, "I'd really like to see me again, too."

He never did.

A single visit to a psychiatrist, of course, failed to bring about a cease-fire between my stepdad and me. Often I looked to my mother for support but received little response. Caught in the cross fire, she was forced eventually to choose between the two of us. "Either you do something with Heather," my stepfather warned, "or I'm leaving."

The prospect of being left alone again with four children overwhelmed my mother. Not knowing what else to do, she made arrangements for me to go stay with my father. By this time he'd finally graduated from a drug-rehabilitation program. I would live with him in a halfway house in Bronx, New York, along with twelve other ex-addicts and their children.

I was thirteen years old. The day after school got out, Mom put me on a plane. I hadn't seen my father in seven years. I was thrilled at the idea of our reunion, but my joy was dimmed by my mother's rejection. She'd done what I'd always feared—she'd chosen the "other man," not only over my father, but over me as well.

Mother's Role: More Crucial Than Ever

Whenever I share events from my childhood, especially the one above, people are appalled. "How could you forgive your mom for sending you away?" they ask.

It wasn't easy. But in time I did come to understand that this was an excruciating decision for her. Back then, she made many difficult decisions. Sometimes her choices helped me. Sometimes they hurt me.

If your father bowed out of your life early, the most important person left on stage was your mother. She had to keep the show going, to make the hard decisions. You looked to her for comfort and guidance in the face of your father's absence, abuse, or neglect.

No wonder Wakerman notes, "A mother attuned to her daughter's needs remains the single most important factor in the girl's subsequent adjustment to father-absence [emotional or physical]."[1]

Many of us who experienced father-loss simultaneously experienced mother-loss. Losing either parent is equally painful and damaging. And to come to terms with your father-loss, you must come to terms with your mother's part in it. Where was your mother while you were losing your father? Did she lessen your pain or increase it?

The women I interviewed for this book answered questions about Mom very differently. Out of their various experiences and stories, however, similar themes arose. Mothers who lose their parenting partners encounter unique problems in raising their children. At times these difficulties overwhelm them.

Three types of "problem" mothers emerged.

The Emotionally Unavailable Mother

This mother missed most of her daughter's emotional cues. She didn't hear her daughter trying to say, "I need you, Mom, to care, to hug me, and show me how to be OK."

This mother typically faced many worries and concerns of her own. Perhaps she worked full-time. Perhaps a new husband demanded her attention, or maybe she was distracted by an alcoholic husband. The hard realities of life depleted her emotional bank and when Daughter tried to make a withdrawal, she came up empty. Mom was physically present, but where her daughter was concerned, she was as absent as Dad.

The Dependent Mother

The dependent mother kept mistaking her role for her daughter's. It was hard to tell who was the child and who was the parent as Mother abandoned her proper place on stage. Daughter attempted to fill in for Mother and in the process lost a portion of her childhood.

Role reversals between mothers and daughters are common, particularly following a husband's death. Amy's father died when she was eleven. Her mother sunk into deep depression and became an alcoholic. Amy's high school years were filled with adult responsibilities rather than cheerleading and football games. Mother was sick. Mother was tired. Mother felt depressed. Amy was nurse, comforter, and mother herself, when all along *she* needed a mother.

The Emotionally Abusive Mother

The emotionally abusive mother delivered lines with a punch. Never at a loss for words, she took center stage and directed her daughter into a corner. She then unleashed upon her child the rage and disappointment she felt with life's injustice, men, and most of all, herself.

Unfortunately, a daughter may receive the brunt of a mother's frustration because she is the closest thing to Mom. A daughter is often viewed by her mother as a reflection of the mother's own self—including her mistakes. Mother in turn punishes herself through her daughter, verbally cutting her down to size—sometimes in front of an audience.

Not all emotional abuse is overt, however. It can be subtle and manipulative. One woman described how her mother always made her wear the most unpopular clothing styles. She appeared to delight in her daughter's discomfort. A mother's abuse can also be verbal or emotional, physical or sexual. Did your mother's performance during your childhood fit any of these roles?

The point is not to categorize or label our mothers, but to be honest about their role in our father-loss. And that's not as easy as it sounds. Rarely does Mother hold a balanced place in the father-deprived daughter's heart. She tends to rise to the position of heroine or stumble into the role of villainess.

The Heroine

A surprising number of father-deprived daughters idealize their mothers. Their mother's mistakes are explained away, their vices too easily understood, their failures glossed over.

Julie's parents divorced when she was eight years old. Her father moved out of state, and her mother went to work as a full-time secretary.

In her twenties, Julie sought counseling for depression. She assured her counselor that she had a "wonderful" mother. After several months, though, Julie's counselor urged her to examine her mother's role more carefully.

"Six weeks later," says Julie, "I called my mom to talk about something important. She was taking a nap and wouldn't come to the phone. When I hung up, I started to cry. And then I got angry. She was always sleeping. Always too tired. All my life she had been taking a nap!

"At my next counseling session," she continues, "all this stuff came out. I was so mad at her! Why didn't she care more? Why didn't she see that I needed help back then? I had to either act like I was sick or misbehave just to get her attention."

At first, it hurt Julie to admit these things about her mother. "But it turned out to be so freeing," she says. "The best part was that I was able to talk about my feelings to my mom. And then I could forgive her."

Why a father-deprived daughter would choose to draw this imaginary picture of a heroine mother is easy to understand. As the sole parent left, Mom is the one she is forced to cling to and identify with while growing up. To admit or say something bad about Mom is to say it about herself.

Also, security is an issue here. If a daughter has already lost Dad, she doesn't want to risk a second rejection. If she lets herself get angry at Mom, who's left?

While growing up, disallowing Mother any faults is an understandable coping strategy. However, in adulthood, a daughter takes a brave step when she acknowledges that maybe Mom wasn't the heroine she'd thought. Yes, she may still fear rejection as much as ever, but only as she's honest about her mother's role can she hope to find healing for her mother-hurts. And only then is she free to fully accept her mother, faults and all.

The Villainess

Not every father-deprived daughter needs to cling to Mom so desperately that she refuses to acknowledge her downfalls. Many have taken the opposite route. More powerful than the need to secure Mom's love was the need to separate from her—especially if the perception of her was already negative.

In divorce, a daughter sometimes views her mother as abandon-able or unlovable. If she can make Mom the villainess, she can blame her for Dad's departure. This diminishes her own feelings of rejection.

Likewise, a mother who tolerates abuse, alcoholism, or some other type of dysfunctional behavior from her husband, or suffers from it herself, may be viewed by her daughter as weak and helpless. This daughter's priority is to *not* identify with her passive, villainous mother.

Much to my mom's dismay, I easily perceived and then remarked on her weaknesses—real and imagined.

I considered her spineless. (She wasn't.) I resented her for not waiting longer for my father and for remarrying. And then

I resented her seeming inability to take my side in my feuds with my stepdad.

I have had to deal with blame and anger toward my mom, just as I had to deal with blame and anger toward my dad. I've had to release her from my judgments and take responsibility for my own life. One night I called her and in essence said: "Mom, you did the best you could with what you had. I'm sorry I blamed so much on you. We were just one big hurting family, weren't we?"

Some of your mothers more than earned your anger or resentment, especially if they stood by while your father abused or neglected you. However, blame carried into adulthood makes the soul bitter. And bitterness keeps you from making peace with your mother and from getting your wounds healed.

The "Other"

Whether you viewed your mother as a heroine, a villainess, or something in between, in the absence of your father through death or divorce, the most important decisions she made were whether or not to remarry and whom to marry, for he would be your new daddy. If mothers are the most important factor in adjustment to father-loss, stepfathers are potentially the most painful. Like the sting of an orange on an open wound is a strange man barging in to take Daddy's place.

I often see sadness in a woman's eyes when I mention her father, but hatred springs to the same woman's eyes at the mention of her stepfather.

Why so much anger, hurt, and resentment toward stepdads? Why are they so rarely successful in developing a loving relationship with their stepdaughters?

Between 1980 and 1990, the number of two-parent homes which contained stepfathers rose 40 percent.[2] In most cases, stepdad enters the scene with the cards already stacked against him. His new daughter feels intensely loyal to her "real" father. She views her stepfather as a threat to that bond; he is the one who has now made her father's return to his rightful position impossible. To top that off, a stepfather is also a threat to the coveted time and attention of Mommy—the only parent the daughter has left.

This isn't to say that stepdads don't do their share of damage to relationships with their stepdaughters. They can be gruff, insensitive, even abusive. More often than not, they view the situation unrealistically; it is difficult to love a hostile, hurting child. And regardless of how a child of divorce or death may appear outwardly, usually her heart is deeply wounded.

There are exceptions to the negative stepfather experience. However, if you're reading this book, it's likely your case isn't one of them. Chances are a stepfather in your past heightened your loss rather than lessened it.

Do you remember that childhood trick where someone would rewrap an empty gum wrapper to make it look as if it hadn't been opened? When you opened it, it was empty. Similarly, our stepfathers looked like dads, and we may even have called them "Daddy," but when we peeled off the outer layers, our souls cried out with disappointment and anger. The hands that disciplined us belonged to a stranger. The harsh voice that commanded us to obey evoked our wrath as often as our cooperation.

My stepfather wasn't and isn't a bad man. He came from an abusive and impoverished family. He never experienced a loving father, and didn't know or understand how to be one himself. Understanding this has helped me to respect his efforts. Today I give him credit for taking on four children who were not his own and for admitting past mistakes. Most of all, I'm thankful he adores my mother. They are still together.

What about your own stepfather? Was he a villain, a monster? Or was he an emotionally and spiritually handicapped man given a challenge greater than he could meet?

The Show Goes On

The "production" of your life has continued, and with passage of time, roles have changed. Many of you now find yourself garbed in the attire of a mother, playing a mother's part. But if it is important to the two-parent daughter to avoid Mom's mistakes, it is even more important to the father-deprived daughter.

Some of you find yourself today, though, in a position more similar to your mother's than you'd like. You've been slapped by divorce or the death of your husband. You sense you have an opportunity to redeem the past with your own children, but instead you find yourself blindly repeating it. You are terrified you are becoming just like your mother.

This is part of the problem with either idealizing or blaming

Mom. Both avenues prevent us from *leaving* her, from distancing ourselves from her mistakes. When we idealize her, we are blind to our mother's failures and are likely to repeat them. When we blame her, we are so busy holding on to her mistakes we can't help but repeat them.

But our mother's inheritance does not have to be ours. Through Christ, we are given a new and better legacy. First Peter 1:3, 4 says, "Praise be to the God and Father of our Lord Jesus Christ! In his great mercy he has given us new birth into a living hope through the resurrection of Jesus Christ from the dead, and into an inheritance that can never perish, spoil or fade—kept in heaven for you."

Living in this hope can change not only our future in heaven but our present day on earth. However, God's inheritance is one we must choose to receive. To do that, we must open our arms wide, which requires that we drop our bag of "mother stuff"—old resentments, grudges, and hurts connected to Mom. We need to accept her, in the full light of honesty.

We'll discuss forgiveness in detail in chapter nine. For now, ask the Holy Spirit for direction. Maybe you need to let your mother off the hook verbally, like I did. Maybe, like Julie, you need to confront her about her part in the past. Many experts advocate such confrontations. But bear in mind two things: Your mother may not respond well to a discussion about her role in certain situations, and you and she may have completely different memories about the nature of the event.

Whether you're struggling to come to terms with suppressed mother-hurts or you've been angry at your mother for years, it will be easier to accept her if you remember that she, too, was once a little girl. She has a background, a series of events and circumstances, hurts and joys, that helped make her who she is today.

Only in the last few years have I started to see my mother as a person. I've always known that she grew up without a father herself, but I never thought much about it. When I began this book, I asked my mom to describe her own father-loss.

My mother explained that her father abandoned their family when she was a toddler. Although she never saw him, she wrote him letters constantly, telling him she loved him, asking him to come home. He never answered any of them.

"I finally decided he must not be getting the letters," she told me. "So when I was twelve, I sent him a letter by registered mail. I got the receipt back with his signature on it. I was crushed."

Your mother, like mine, probably took few bows on the stage of life and found heartache more familiar than joy. When you lost a father, she lost a husband. As we understand that our mothers were neither heroines nor villainesses, but hurting, fallible women like ourselves, we can make peace with the part they played in our father-loss.

Time to Consider

God is the Father to the fatherless, but is he a mother to the motherless? Can he comfort us with a mother's love?

Isaiah 66:12-13 reads: "For this is what the Lord says: 'I will extend peace to her like a river, and the wealth of nations like a flooding stream; you will nurse and be carried on her arm and dandled on her knees. *As a mother comforts her child, so will I comfort you;* And you will be comforted over Jerusalem'" (italics added).

1. In what ways did you view your mother as a heroine or a villainess as you grew up?

2. How did your mother's role affect your father-loss? How did she comfort or help you? How did she make things harder?

3. How did your mother respond to, treat, and talk about your father? How did that influence your views of men in general?

4. Proverbs 30:11 says, "There are those who curse their fathers and do not bless their mothers." In what ways, if any, do you still curse your stepfather (if you had one) in your heart? How are you still blaming your mother for the past, instead of blessing her?

5. What can you do now to reconcile past hurts in your relationship with your mother?

My Brother, My Sister

$\mathcal{R}$emember the story of my father wanting to take me and my brother on a train trip? I didn't mention my older sister, Kathy, then nine, in that story. Why not? Because my dad didn't ask her to come—a rejection that hardly slipped past her.

When I recently asked my sister what she remembered about this incident, I could still hear the hurt in her voice. "Did you know that Dad didn't want me to come on that trip? He only wanted you and Jimmy."

A parent can cause immeasurable damage to a child through one simple act. If the train incident was a point of loss for me, it was even more so for Kathy. My father might as well have said, "Kathy, I don't want you with me. I don't love you as much as I love your brother and sister."

Not that Jimmy wasn't injured that day. For years afterward, he was terrified of police. He would cry and scream whenever he heard sirens of any kind. "They're coming! They're coming!" I still remember his panicked wails, especially when he saw flashing lights.

At the time I thought my brother was ridiculous. But I couldn't bring myself to tease him about it. Perhaps, even as a child, I sensed his pain and realized it was mine, too. Somehow we were all in this thing together. For better and, more often, for worse.

Pick-Up Sticks

My oldest son, Noah, loved to play pick-up sticks when he was younger. The game is simple. A pile of colored plastic sticks are dumped onto the floor, and whoever can pick up the most sticks without disturbing the others wins. As you can imagine, many disputes arose as to whether a stick moved or not. "I saw the blue one wiggle," one of the kids was sure to shout.

Unless you grew up an only child, you experienced father-loss not in a vacuum but among your siblings. Tumbled together in a pile of hurts and joys, doubts and fears, you spent your childhood inextricably connected to your siblings. Every word and gesture affected the others.

At times your siblings eased your pain. At other times they increased it. You loved them. You hated them. No matter what, you couldn't help but be touched by your mutual struggle for survival.

In the previous chapter, we asked the question, where was your mother while you were losing your father? Now, other questions are necessary: where were your siblings while you were losing your father? Where are you in relationship to them today?

Storybook Siblings

I've never liked the story of Hansel and Gretel. But it's not the deception of a candy house that bothers me, nor is it the witch who is wicked enough to eat children. It comes earlier than that; it is the idea of a father who succumbed to his wife's persuasion to abandon his children in the woods. Even as a child, that part horrified me.

Yet after Hansel and Gretel escape the witch and are reunited with their father, they forgive him without flinching.

Such simple, happy endings are rare in real life. Instead, those of us whose fathers failed us feel the sting of their rejection long afterward. Many years later we may still find it difficult to forgive.

And how did Hansel and Gretel respond to each other? One version of the Brothers Grimm tale explains that when they woke up, it was night. Gretel was frightened by the dark, so Hansel comforted her. Later, Gretel returns the favor by saving her brother from the witch through an act of sheer bravery.

Such mutual concern and dedication in the face of abandonment and betrayal is touching. For some—those who found in their siblings comfort and loyalty amid the pain of father-loss—the actions of Hansel and Gretel ring true. For others, Hansel and Gretel's cooperative love is a far cry from the reality of their own sibling relationships while growing up. What if Hansel had blamed Gretel for their predicament? What if he'd said, "Gretel, you always did eat too much of the food at home"? And what if Gretel had abandoned Hansel in the cage to get revenge for the time he locked her in the closet when she was three?

A more realistic ending to this story might read: "And Hansel forgave his father, but Gretel never could. She felt Hansel had always been his favorite anyway. Gretel married at a young age, and she and Hansel haven't spoken since."

Pulled Together or Torn Apart?

Siblings within the same family react very differently to their father-loss. Two sisters rarely view their dad, or the loss of him, in the same light. Some sets of siblings pull together and develop intense loyalty in the face of father-loss, as did Hansel and Gretel. Others fragment and fall apart, and permanent chasms settle between siblings.

Many factors determine whether siblings will eventually unite or disperse. However, father-loss does place a unique strain on sibling relationships. When Dad is emotionally or physically absent, sibling rivalry is stepped up, rigid roles are taken on, and the fine line between love and hate becomes even thinner.

Stepped-Up Rivalry

If your father was absent or ineffective, less parental love and affection was available. And because a parent's love is the most prized goal of sibling rivalry, father-loss raises the stakes considerably in sibling competitions.

If you lost your dad to death or divorce, it was as though a frantic warning rang out among the kids, "Mom's the only one left! Get her time and attention now because it's in even shorter supply than before!"

If your father was physically present but emotionally absent, feelings of sibling rivalry probably still increased. With little of Dad's time, attention, and approval to go around, the scramble for it likely became more intense. When sibling rivalry steps up, so does the importance of Mom's or Dad's response to it.

Parents can calm competitions and bring balance to a tense situation, or they can compound the problem by showing preference.

A parent who shows favoritism toward one child in an already strong sibling rivalry is tossing a match onto a gas-soaked log. The destructive fires of jealousy and dissension blaze forth instantly and are difficult to put out.

After Beth's parents' divorce, her father would send her sister money and birthday gifts, but Beth received nothing. "I still resent my sister for that," she says, "even though I know it wasn't her fault."

Such obvious acts of favoritism, whether intentional or not, are common. The effects are powerful, not due to the value of the birthday card or the money, but because these things represent love and favor to a child.

If rivalry was stepped up in your home, so was the potential for deep splits between you and your siblings. In healthy families, the parents' judicial wisdom eases sibling competition. In families that are hurting because of father-loss, the sibling motto often becomes "Every child for himself." Such unobstructed rivalry can destroy relationships and drag into adulthood.

Role Playing

A father is like an umbrella of protection over his family. When he is absent or neglects his fatherly duties, the family loses some of its protection from life's storms. As family members begin to "get wet" and each child scrambles to stay out of the rain, they may assume new roles to survive. These roles can become unhealthy, or "dysfunctional," when they restrict a child's range of "acceptable" emotions and behaviors.

Sally was the oldest in a family of five children. After her dad died when she was ten, she made an admirable attempt to hold an umbrella over the family. She took on more than her share of household duties and tried to keep her younger siblings from getting into trouble. No one recognized that the umbrella was too heavy, or that when a storm hit, she suffered the most. Sally is what psychiatrists term a "parentified" child.

You and your siblings might have taken on one of many roles to compensate for Dad's absence. Sometimes these roles were mutually beneficial. Sometimes they were self-preserving and pitted you against one another. Dr. Norm Wright lists ten dysfunctional roles in his book, *Always Daddy's Girl.* Do you recognize yourself or your siblings in any one or more of the following?

"The Doer" takes on more than her share of family responsibility. She resents this, but her busyness makes her feel important and needed by the family.

"The Enabler" wants peace at any cost, not realizing that she makes it possible for dysfunctional or addictive behavior to continue. This role is especially prevalent in alcoholic homes.

"The Loner" reacts to family problems by withdrawing into herself. She rarely expresses her feelings and often feels distant from parents and siblings.

"The Hero" wants to impress and please others but too often at her own expense. Often oldest children are heroes.

They get the best grades and bring home the achievement awards, but they can't find or please themselves.

"The Mascot" is the clown or comedian and relieves the family tensions by keeping everyone laughing. He or she uses this behavior to get attention and cover up feelings.

"The Manipulator" subtly controls the family. This child knows how to get his or her way through various acts and ploys.

"The Critic" sees the negative in everyone and everything—and never hesitates to voice an opinion.

"The Scapegoat" gets into more than his or her share of trouble; this child is blamed for many of the family's problems.

"Daddy's Little Princess" or "Mommy's Little Man" is exalted to a favored position in the family in order to meet a parent's emotional needs.

"The Saint" is expected to be the "spiritual" one in the family and feels compelled to fulfill that role. She may feel guilty about her normal desires that seem "unspiritual."[1]

To find an exact label for you and your siblings isn't necessary. What is important is that you recognize how your family interacted in the midst of father-loss. You may have played more than one role. I was a manipulator, a critic, and a scapegoat. How did your role affect your relationship with your brothers and sisters? Did role-playing unite or divide you as a sibling group?

The Fine Line

As mentioned earlier in this chapter, in sibling relationships where father-loss has occurred there may be a fine line between love and hate. Without a loving father to lead the troops and unite hearts, emotional needs may be intensified. Like Hansel and Gretel, you and your siblings may have looked to each other for love, comfort, and support, especially when the woods grew dark.

And yet, your siblings may also have served as a "pin-cushion" of sorts. They were handy when you needed to act out your frustrations and hurts. You could hate them today and know they'd be around to hate some more the next morning.

This "fine line" is in effect in almost any sibling relationship. However, in the case of father-loss, when siblings are caught up in a joint struggle for survival, identity, and security, the line between love and hate is stretched so thin that it sometimes disappears.

My brother Jimmy and I are only a year and a half apart. As kids, we fought like crazy over anything and everything. Through parental intervention, my brother often won his way. I'd stare in disgust at his scrawny form, at the way his goofy cowlick stuck up, and the way his glasses sat on his face cock-eyed. Oftentimes I could hardly gulp down the hatred I felt for him. And I know he felt the same way about me.

Once, when I was sixteen, my stepfather and I got into an ugly row about my oft-broken curfew. Afterward, he stormed upstairs and yelled at my mom that he wanted me "out of the house." He'd had enough of my sarcasm, rebellion, and disrespect.

I heard Jimmy go up to their bedroom and interrupt their conversation. "I know she's horrible," I heard him say to my stepdad. "And I know she makes you mad. She makes me mad, too!" His voice rose with emotion so that I could hear his words clearly as I stood on the landing below their bedroom. "And I hate her, too!" he screamed. "But I still love her. She's my sister, and you can't kick her out!"

What was he saying? Shock and disbelief stunned me. I slumped against the stair railing, my eyes filling with tears. My brother, whom I'd tormented, was actually defending me!

In the battle between this brother and sister, the smoke was clearing and the war was almost over. Jimmy and I ended up on the side of love.

Did you and your siblings cross back and forth over the thin line between love and hate? Did the effects of father-loss stretch that line even thinner? On which side did you end up? Does it even matter? What's a sibling worth, anyway?

The Value of a Sibling

Have you ever considered how much *time* you spent with your siblings growing up? Together you experienced idle minutes in the backseat of the family car, dragging moments at the grocery checkout counter, thousands of mealtimes, not to mention the hours spent fighting over the imaginary line drawn down the middle of the bed.

Possibly never again in our lives will we spend such concentrated amounts of time with another person. For this reason, few know us as intimately as our siblings. And none could know and understand the heartaches of our shared childhoods the way our brothers and sisters do.

We've all heard about victims who develop a special bond with each other through tragic or catastrophic circumstances. Many of you endured traumatic childhoods and developed that unique bond in your relationship with your siblings.

Many sibling bonds, however, are severed rather than strengthened by father-loss, tragedy, or dysfunction. In the process of losing Daddy, one or more siblings are lost.

Recently, I caught a segment on the news about a chain-reaction drowning. As three California teenagers walked on a frozen lake, the ice broke and they fell in. Two adults nearby tried to save them. They fell in, too. Next, a forest ranger and another adult attempted a rescue. In the end, seven people drowned in icy waters.

I stared in horror at the television as I watched the coverage of trained divers searching for the dead bodies. I wished vainly that they might still find some survivors. But, no, it was too late.

When father-loss takes place, the foundation of the family shatters and breaks. All the members fall in. Grasping for life in icy waters, siblings try to save each other—and themselves. In the confusion, sometimes a sibling sinks beneath the ice. Sometimes an entire family is submerged, never to regain wholeness.

What about your family? Perhaps you've lost contact with a sibling, or your relationship with him or her is estranged. Maybe you feel separated from your siblings by a cold chasm of indifference or apathy.

Unlike the ice accident, it is never too late to toss in a line, to forgive, or to reach out and grab a sibling's hand. Can you let go of your resentments? Can you forget who got rescued, who didn't, who pulled the others down, who got special treatment?

Of course, this doesn't guarantee a loving reunion or that the sibling you reach out to will reciprocate. But isn't a sibling worth fighting for, worth the risk of creeping across the ice? What if, in your search for a father, you rediscover the value of a brother or sister?

Time to Consider

1. How did father-loss increase feelings of rivalry between you and your siblings? Has the rivalry continued? What are you doing to bring healing?

2. How did you and your siblings respond differently to father-loss? What roles did you take on in order to cope? What are you doing to break unhealthy patterns?

3. Describe any jealousies you felt toward your siblings. How did you, or will you, overcome them?

4. If you have more than one sibling, who are you closest to and why? Who fell under the ice? Are any attempts being made to rescue that person(s)?

5. What part did your father and mother play in your sibling relationships? How did they help or hurt?

6. God is aware of the fine line between sibling hate and love. Proverbs 18:19 says, "An offended brother is more unyielding than a fortified city, and disputes are like the barred gates of a citadel." But Proverbs 17:17 says, "A friend loves at all times, and a brother is born for adversity." On which side of the line did you and your siblings end up? Why? If on the hate side, what can you do to change it?

Who Am I?

*M*y stay in the Bronx with my father was short-lived and disappointing. I could tell my dad was glad to have me with him. But when he came home from work at night, he'd only say a quick hello and then disappear into his room. He'd sit alone in the dark for hours.

Sometimes he'd leave his door cracked a bit. From down the hall, I would watch the orange glow of his cigarette moving up and down in the blackness. I wondered what he was thinking so much about and why, now that I was here with him, I still felt alone.

I'd lived with my dad for only three months when my mother called to say I could come home. She and my stepdad, she explained, had never intended to leave me with my father permanently.

I arrived home in time for the new school year. But little changed between me and my stepfather. We resumed our war with aplomb.

Meanwhile, in New York, my father sank into a deep depression. He lost his job and within a year began to abuse drugs again.

The following spring, without a dime in his pocket, he

decided to hitchhike across the country to see us kids. He phoned frequently as he progressed, and the closer he got to Washington, the more we noticed signs of mental illness again. He predicted that a great flood would end the world in June. Then, in Colorado, police arrested him and threw him in jail. His crime was harassing people in a Dairy Queen because they wouldn't believe he was God.

Three weeks later, I arrived home from school to find my dad waiting for me in the front yard. He wore a ridiculous pair of red and blue bowling shoes. His long, dirty hair hung over his face, and his brown polyester pants were at least two inches too short.

When he saw me, he called my name with a catch in his voice, as if he might cry, "Heather!"

"Hi, Dad," I said, approaching slowly.

He grabbed me almost violently and hugged me close. His disheveled clothes smelled like something had died and rotted in the pockets. I resisted the urge to pull away and tried not to breathe in.

I'd grown up clinging to the good in my father. I wanted desperately to feel proud of this tormented man who was my daddy. I liked to remind myself that he had a master's degree in environmental science from Rutgers University. That sounded so intelligent.

But now, for the first time, I let myself feel shame. And I wondered, *If this is my father, what does that make me?*

Tell Me Who I Am, Daddy

If I'd ever had to answer "Who am I?" at age fourteen, I would have said, "I'm a brat, the daughter of a lunatic, and my family hates me."

Although I'd answer this question differently today, I still struggle with self-esteem. And I'd probably still mention my father at some point. Why?

Psychologists say that our identity is largely based on "where we came from." For this reason, our view of, and feelings toward, our fathers greatly influence our self-concepts.

For example, if your father was a staggering alcoholic, and if you became disillusioned with him in any way, you probably transferred some of the shame you felt toward him back onto yourself.

If you never knew your father, or where he was, you may have grown up feeling you had no identity or you were only half a person.

The daughter of the divorced father often feels that her identity, her foundation, has shattered. I talked to one woman who said, "Still today, if my parents got back together and loved each other, I would finally feel like I knew who I was."

If your dad died while you were young, his absence affected your self-concept, since it is difficult to identify with a dead father. Many daughters whose fathers die while they are young irrationally conclude, *If only he'd loved me more, he would have found a way to live.*

Tell Me What I'm Worth, Daddy

Children need to know not only who they are but how *valuable* they are. To feel valuable, they must feel special.

Whenever I take my youngest son, Nathan, to the doctor, he's anxious to get on the scales. He smirks while the nurse fiddles with the knobs and slides the metal bar across the scale. When she announces the exact number of pounds he weighs, a look of satisfaction crosses his face. How much does *he* weigh? How tall is *he*?

Children rely on Mom and Dad to communicate their value through everyday words and actions. Dad's role is especially important because he is sometimes (though not always) seen as the one who represents to his daughter not only the world of males but often the world of business—the world "out there." His influence is so great that one respected researcher noted, "A good predictor of an adolescent girl's mental health is her relationship with her father."[1]

What happens when an absent or ineffective father doesn't affirm his daughter? An empty, needy place is created in her spirit. She often spends years trying to fill that void, looking for proof of her value.

Years ago, I watched Phil Donahue interview Audrey Hepburn on his show. She solemnly related stories from her tragic childhood in Holland. The Nazis had invaded her country, and her family endured five years under German occupation. She lost close relatives in the war and witnessed Jews being rounded up and pushed onto cattle trucks.

"This must have left you very insecure," Donahue noted.

Without hesitation Hepburn answered, "That is not what left me insecure. My father leaving us left me insecure—for life, perhaps."

Hepburn's parents divorced when she was ten. Her father entered the war and never came home. "I was terribly jealous of other little girls who had adoring daddies and all that," she said.

To imagine this stately, accomplished woman feeling insecure is difficult. But her words testify to the important role a father plays in developing security and self-confidence in his daughter.

In her autobiography, *Commitment to Love*, Deanna McClary shares how her father, a recovering alcoholic, diminished her self-esteem while she grew up. "I believed truth came out of a drunk man's mouth, that the liquor made him say what he really thought. So when Daddy, whom I loved, said I was ugly or stupid, I believed him," she writes.

"Relatives and people at church and school and in the neighborhood began telling me that I was pretty when I was still a little girl. I didn't understand it; I couldn't understand it. I didn't know then, though it's popularly accepted psychological truth now, but my self-image, my self-worth, my entire sense of self was completely wrapped up in what I believed my father thought of me."[2]

McClary's story illustrates how even after a daughter has left home and appears to have found success and confidence, she may still feel inferior inside. She continues to measure her worth by her father's scale.

When Nathan steps on the doctor's scale, he gets affirmed.

In your childhood, what happened when you stepped on your father's scale and looked up at his face?

If your father was absent, you probably decided you weren't valuable enough to weigh into his life at all. You measured a big zero.

If your dad was neglectful, you may have felt that he declared you unimportant, almost weightless.

If your father was abusive, he may have thought so little of you that he lashed out in anger and knocked you right off the scales.

I have a beautiful, talented friend who was deeply hurt by her father. In fact, he is still hurting her today by his lack of interest in her life. "I don't think I'll ever get over the rejection I feel from him," she says. "Something inside will always doubt my worth and lovableness."

My friend is still in search of self-esteem. She is still jumping on and off her father's scale, waiting for him to value her. What hope can she and others like her embrace?

Self-Esteem: A Slippery Subject

When a person suffers from appendicitis, a surgeon removes the organ and sews up the wound. The results are clean-cut and obvious. If only an inferiority complex were as easy to "fix."

Self-esteem is a slippery, complex subject. Much of the advice we receive only touches the surface and doesn't change our inner being.

I am very much "in process" in this area. In my head I know I am a valuable person, priceless to God. But my search for self-esteem, like my friend's, is laden with slippery places. Part of me still feels like that little girl who missed her daddy's train. And part of me is still trying to forget the stench of my mentally ill father's embrace.

I know I am not alone. You ache with doubt like I do. You, too, missed out on the affirmation that a father brings.

So how *do* we fulfill our search for self-esteem? Perhaps the only way to fulfill the search is to redefine what it truly is.

It's difficult to grab hold of self-esteem because so many counterfeits along the way confuse us. When we actively search for ways to feel better about ourselves, we typically do things like buy nice clothes, embark on a new career, or try to impress our friends.

We may capture a degree of satisfaction in this pursuit. We may have fleeting moments of reprieve. But a closer look often reveals that we have snared ego, selfishness, or pride instead of self-esteem. So our search continues.

What does the Bible say about self-esteem? We don't find this word combination in Scripture, but the subject is addressed often.

Paul wrote to the Philippians, "Do nothing out of selfish ambition or vain conceit, but in humility consider others better than yourselves" (Phil 2:3).

The apostle Paul had a host of reasons to feel good about himself. "If anyone else thinks he has reasons to put confidence in the flesh, I have more: circumcised on the eighth day, of the people of Israel, of the tribe of Benjamin, a

Hebrew of Hebrews; in regard to the law, a Pharisee; as for zeal, persecuting the church; as for legalistic righteousness, faultless" (Phil 3:4-6).

If Paul had lived in our culture, he might have said, "I am a wealthy Kennedy by birth, I've driven a Mercedes, I've held high political office, and I'm good-looking."

While Paul had reason to feel good in society's eyes, he had reason to feel ashamed in God's eyes. He'd relentlessly persecuted God's church and had approved the deaths of many Christians. In his own words, "I am less than the least of all God's people" (Eph 3:8).

Was Paul in search of self-esteem? No. Paul was a man in search of God, and in the process, discovered a greater fulfillment and purpose.

"But whatever was to my profit I now consider loss for the sake of Christ. What is more, I consider everything a loss compared to the surpassing greatness of knowing Christ Jesus my Lord, for whose sake I have lost all things. I consider them rubbish, that I may gain Christ and be found in him, not having a righteousness of my own that comes from the law, but that which is through faith in Christ—the righteousness that comes from God and is by faith" (Phil 3:7-9).

Where do you run when suddenly you don't know who you are and you don't feel valuable?

Paul ran to God. He did two things we can imitate. First, he "lost all things" and counted them as "rubbish" (Phil 3:8). He wasn't looking to the world for self-esteem. Second, he pressed on to know God as fully as possible, to obtain all that God had for him.

"Not that I have already obtained all this, or have already been made perfect, but I press on to take hold of that for which Christ Jesus took hold of me. Brothers, I do not consider myself yet to have taken hold of it. But one thing I do: *Forgetting what is behind and straining toward what is ahead, I press on toward the goal to win the prize for which God has called me heavenward in Christ Jesus*" (Phil 3:12-14, italics added).

You too can forget what lies behind, what your father said or didn't say. Press on toward the goal of self-esteem. Step up on God's scales, look into his face, and let him reexplain love and acceptance to your heart.

The Heavenly Father's Scales

Just as you identified with your earthly father and found disappointment, you can reidentify with your heavenly Father and find hope.

God's scales are the only ones that weigh correctly.

Did your alcoholic father call you stupid? God says you are skillfully and wonderfully made. In him you have the mind of Christ. Wisdom, which is more valuable than intelligence, is yours for the asking. (See Psalm 139:14; 1 Corinthians 2:16; James 1:5.)

Did your father drop out of your life after your parents' divorce, leaving you feeling unimportant and "weightless"? God says you are a treasured possession, part of a royal priesthood, and that his thoughts for and about you are as many as the sands. (See Deuteronomy 7:6; Psalm 139:18; 1 Peter 2:9.)

Did you ever feel close to your father? Or was he cold and distant, so that you thirsted for love but were never satisfied? God the Father desires such closeness with you that he wants to live inside you. If you've given your life to him, you need never be thirsty or empty again. (See John 17:23; 4:13, 14.)

Did your father die while you were young, making you feel incomplete and abandoned? You are complete in God the Father. He is the Father to the fatherless. He is all that you need, and he will never abandon you. (See Colossians 2:10; Hebrews 13:5.)

Imagine God's pain when we desperately search the world over for self-esteem. All the while, he waits for us to look to him.

Our earthly fathers let us down. They left on trains and didn't return. They showed up in red and blue bowling shoes. But God will never disappoint us, and those who hope in him will never be put to shame.

Time to Consider

1. Answer the question, "Who am I?" based solely on your interaction (or lack of interaction) with your father.

2. Answer the same question based on your relationship with God.

3. Where have you searched for self-esteem and not found it (e.g., career, kids, husband, possessions, etc.)? How has that made you feel?

4. What steps are you taking to find self-esteem in your relationship with God?

5. Study Psalm 139. How does this psalm speak to you about your unique value on God's scales?

It Still Hurts

*I*f you were sexually abused by your father or stepfather, not only did you not have a daddy, but you were betrayed and defiled by the one who should have functioned as your protector.

We've all seen the bandage commercial that claims to "stop the hurting." If only your wounds could be healed as easily. Instead, they go so deep you may have attempted to suppress them altogether. Despite your efforts to numb or ignore the pain, it still hurts.

One in four women are sexually abused by the time they reach age eighteen. This figure includes all categories of offenders—strangers, neighbors, brothers, uncles, and unfortunately, many fathers and even mothers.

The *New American Heritage Dictionary* describes incest as "sexual intercourse between persons who are so closely related that their marriage is illegal or forbidden by custom." Sexual abuse is a broader term. The offender is not necessarily a relative, and the abuse can take many forms. It doesn't always involve physical contact.

Dr. Regina McGlothlin has counseled many sexual abuse and incest victims. She gives the following example of a common type of sexual abuse, exhibitionism, which is not always recognized as such: "A man is baby-sitting children. He takes a shower and puts on the man-of-the-house's robe. He sits in view of the children and conveniently lets the robe fall open to expose his genitals. The children may notice rapid breathing or an erection. They sense something isn't right, and they feel afraid and confused. That's abuse."[1]

Sexual abuse, no matter how subversive, is always powerful because it involves not just the physical but also the emotional and spiritual. Violation of a person's spirit takes place whenever sexual abuse occurs, even in its most subtle form. For this reason, what looks like an isolated act can have enormous repercussions later in life.

Take Leslie, for instance. After marrying, Leslie had difficulty responding sexually to her husband. "I felt angry and violated whenever we made love," she says. "Over a period of years, my counselor concluded that I must have experienced sexual abuse as a child. I insisted I hadn't."

Meanwhile, Leslie noticed that after returning from each visit with her mother and stepfather, who lived out of state, her problems with sex increased.

"Finally, my stepfather's voyeurism came to light. The entire time I was growing up, he was spying on me through a hole in the knotty-pine wall of my bedroom.

"I'd discovered that hole as a child," she explains, "but I'd accused my brother of making it because it led into his bedroom. I never thought about the fact that his room was once my stepdad's workroom. No wonder I couldn't stand for my stepdad to touch me!"

Leslie was never physically violated, but she was sexually abused nonetheless. She grew up in an unhealthy atmosphere of sexual perversion. She *felt* violated in her spirit, even though at first she could not pinpoint an offense.

If you suffered sexual abuse or incest as a child, know that you are not alone, strange, or different. You are in the company of a massive number of women.

Second, know that you are not in the remotest way responsible for what happened to you. The child is never at fault.

Third, recognize that you need more help than you can find in this chapter. Seek counseling with a highly recommended and experienced therapist or a trusted Christian counselor.

With these objectives in mind, here is one woman's story. She echoes thousands more.

Melanie

Melanie lives with her husband and two-year-old daughter in a large country house decorated in shades of pink. At first, I was a bit nervous about talking with Melanie. I knew she was a survivor of sexual abuse, but she had never "spilled" her story to anyone before. How much would she want to tell me? How much did I want to know?

There is no "typical" abuse story, but to help you identify similar experiences, I've divided Melanie's story into stages.

The Circumstances

Melanie never knew her birth-father. She called her step-father Daddy and had always considered him that—even though he often beat her. The physical abuse began at age seven, and the sexual abuse began at age ten. She knew before he ever touched her that something wasn't right, that something evil lurked inside of him.

Because her mother worked as a waitress at night, she and her siblings were often left alone with their stepdad. One night, as she lay on the living room floor coloring, she felt her stepfather staring at her. She turned around, but she couldn't understand what she saw in his eyes. It made her feel nervous and uncomfortable.

Her stepdad's attitude toward her changed. But she couldn't have known what lay ahead.

The Crime

On the nights her mother worked, Melanie tucked her younger sister into her parents' bed at night. Melanie stayed with her until she fell asleep.

One night, Melanie fell asleep, too. The next thing she knew, her stepfather was lying on top of her. She didn't know what was happening. At first, she thought he was going to smother her. She was terrified.

She had absolutely no idea what sex was. Afterward, she sat on the floor of the bathroom and sobbed. The next day, though, she tried to act normal. She didn't tell anyone.

The Cover-Up

People who have never experienced sexual abuse often ask victims, "Why didn't you tell someone?" They are incredulous that a person could be silent in the face of abuse. They don't understand how abusers use fear and intimidation to control their victims.

Melanie's stepfather never overtly threatened her. But she knew that if she told anyone, she'd get hit. She'd be in big trouble. As the sexual abuse continued, her stepdad bribed her by taking her to the store. Whatever Melanie wanted, Melanie could have. He bought her silence.

Shame is another reason children fail to speak up in instances of abuse. Dr. McGlothlin says, "Children are ego-centric. They see the world as revolving around them. If they sense that something is bad or wrong, they automatically take responsibility for it."

One night when Melanie was twelve she listened to Billy Graham talk about sex on television. It began to dawn on her that this was what her stepfather was doing to her. But according to Billy Graham, sex was beautiful, God-made, and clean.

"I thought, 'Oh, good! Maybe I'm not so ugly and horrible after all,'" Melanie said. "Of course, I'd missed the part when he connected sex to marriage."

And even though she heard him say those things, she still felt ashamed, ugly, and worthless. And she knew she couldn't tell anyone.

The Cry for Help

Many sexual abuse victims never move past the cover-up to cry out for help. Melanie might not have either, had she not encountered an approachable adult.

One day when she was in the sixth grade, an uncle showed up at the door. She hadn't even known he existed. His wife, for some reason, seemed more like a friend than other adults. Melanie and the woman were alone in Melanie's bedroom visiting when, out of nowhere, Melanie began to cry. "Is he supposed to be doing this to me?" she sobbed to the older woman.

The woman made Melanie sit down and tell her in detail what happened. Within hours they were down at the courthouse, and the police had arrested Melanie's stepdad.

Melanie did the right thing. She told someone! Surely help was on the way. But it wasn't. Children are often disbelieved when they speak up about abuse.

The Cross Examination

Melanie was taken to the doctor for a physical exam and then to the courthouse where they asked her all kinds of questions. She wasn't prepared, and she felt traumatized.

Her stepfather denied everything. He took a lie detector test, and it claimed he was telling the truth. Then the doctor said Melanie's hymen wasn't broken. Apparently, he hadn't ever fully penetrated her.

Melanie was sitting on a bench outside the courtroom the first time she saw her mother after all this. Her mom sat down beside Melanie, glared into her eyes, and said, "You liar! How dare you make up something like this! You're just trying to get attention, you witch."

Melanie knew then that it was over. No one believed her.

The Crossroad

When a sexual abuse victim cries out for help, an important crossroad is reached. The child should be immediately removed from the offender's presence and receive counseling and help. In Melanie's case, this didn't happen. Melanie returned home, branded a liar and stripped of self-esteem.

Her stepfather never sexually touched her again. But the beatings escalated. He hit harder and more often; he hated her vehemently after his abusiveness was confronted.

We find a similar account in the Bible. Amnon raped his half-sister Tamar and afterwards "hated her with intense hatred. In fact, he hated her more than he had loved her. Amnon said to her, 'Get up and get out!'" (2 Sm 13:15).

Melanie embodied her stepdad's shameful sin. He hated her more than ever now because she was a daily reminder that he was not only a sex offender but a liar.

A few verses later in Tamar's story her brother Absalom asked her, "'Has that Amnon, your brother, been with you? Be quiet now, my sister; he is your brother. Don't take this thing to heart.' And Tamar lived in her brother Absalom's house, a desolate woman" (2 Sm 13:20).

Tamar, too, was instructed to cooperate in a "cover-up." And the word *desolate* not only fits Tamar but Melanie as well. Life went on without either love or care. Melanie had no friends and felt totally alone. She simply accepted that this was her life, and that she was unimportant.

When Melanie was sixteen, her mother contracted cancer. Even though she hadn't believed Melanie about the abuse,

Melanie had always clung to her mother as the one stable, unchanging thing in her life. Now she was dying. In the hospital, she took Melanie's hand and for the first time told her daughter that she loved her.

Melanie's mother passed away the following day. By that time, Melanie had made one friend who happened to come from a Christian home. Melanie was allowed to live with them.

God intervened in Melanie's life at this point. She accepted the Lord as her Savior and soon afterward met the man who would become her husband. They married when she was eighteen.

"Mark was sent from God," she said as we closed our interview. "What would I have done without him?"

Looking at Melanie's tear-streaked face, I couldn't escape the feeling that we'd just unplugged an emotional dam, one that appeared to hold anything but healed waters. It would be difficult to plug back up. My heart was heavy.

Two weeks later I spoke to the friend who had originally put me in touch with Melanie. "Melanie hasn't been the same since you two talked. She seems so upset and says she just can't get herself back together."

Obviously our interview had reopened an incredibly painful wound for Melanie. I prayed she'd get the help she needed.

Soon afterward, I received good news from our mutual friend: Melanie had sought counseling to overcome her sexual abuse. She was already making progress.

Three months later, I got together with Melanie again.

But this time her face—her entire countenance—seemed

changed. She wanted to let me know that, yes, women who have suffered sexual abuse do need counseling, even if they think they don't.

Dr. McGlothlin echoes Melanie's observation. "A person almost always needs counseling, someone to carefully take them through the healing process. People try to go around it, under it, or suppress it. But the only way to get out of pain is to go right through the center of it."[2]

Through extensive prayer, counseling, and the reading of several books, Melanie is passing through the pain and coming out the other side. "It still hurts," she says, "but not anything like before.

"I used to think something was wrong with me," she says, "I'd been told I was an angry woman. That was true. And I've always had a hard time making friends. I felt abnormal and strange. Now I know that I'm normal, considering what I've gone through."

Melanie described how she has never felt truly loved by God. She'd always thought she had to pull his strings to make him love her. She had never let God touch her hurting places or felt "good enough" for him. Now she knows she's OK with God as she is. For the first time in her Christian life, she can relax and let God love her.

Toward the end of our conversation, Melanie said to me, "I can't believe I waited twenty years to do this. I've just been surviving, going through the motions. Now I can really live."

I hear Christ's words echoed in hers. "I have come that they may have life, and have it to the full" (Jn 10:10).

Time to Consider

Assuming you've been sexually abused in some way:

1. If you've never told anyone what happened to you, what keeps you from doing so?

2. How do you feel today toward the person who abused you?

3. Why do you think the abuse happened to you? First, allow your "little girl" to answer. Second, answer as the objective adult you are today. Do you carry any false guilt or shame? How are you dealing with that?

4. What aspects of Melanie's experience did you relate to the most? What kind of help are you getting?

5. How much do you blame God for your sexual abuse? Can you express this anger to him?

Can I Cry Now?

*E*ventually my dad lost or discarded the red and blue bowling shoes. But in another sense, he never took them off.

Although his delusions of grandeur passed, for the next nine years he battled drug addiction, depression, and schizophrenic tendencies. He traveled from town to town, shuffling in and out of hospitals, missions, and halfway houses.

He became increasingly suicidal as I entered adulthood. Once he tried to kill himself by swallowing a razor blade. Another time he drank rubbing alcohol. Most often, he overdosed on drugs. These attempts were not only cries for help, they were his tickets into "real" hospitals versus the mental hospitals.

So when I received a phone call on Memorial Day informing me that my dad had attempted suicide again, I wasn't alarmed. Within hours he'd be complaining about the food and demanding that Tom and I bring him a carton of cigarettes.

But when I phoned the hospital a half hour later, the emergency room nurse sounded serious. "Honey," she said, "you'd better come quickly. I don't know if your dad is going to make it."

Her words set off a fluttering of panic in my chest. No one had ever said that to me before. Sometimes doctors or nurses had called simply to find out where my dad belonged or to obtain his history, but they'd never talked to me as if I really mattered—or as if he did, either.

My father was in an Oregon hospital. I was the only one of us kids living in that state. Tom and I drove an hour to get there. By the time we arrived, my father's heart had already stopped twice. Seven hospital personnel were doing everything possible to save him.

I became hysterical and frantically begged Tom, "Get Kathy here right now." My sister was a five-hour drive away in Washington. While Tom called her, an orderly led me into a small room to wait.

Fifteen minutes later, a heavyset nurse approached. "I'm sorry." She put her arm firmly around my back. "We tried, but we couldn't save him. Your father died."

My knees buckled and a moan escaped my chest. I sobbed and questioned the nurse for details, convinced that this couldn't really be happening. It was too much like television—except I hadn't stood by my dad's bed and told him I loved him.

Many of my friends and relatives had always figured my dad's death would be a relief. Feeling the burden of his instability the last five years, I, too, had often thought it might be better. I had even learned to laugh about it, because it hurt too much to cry. But then, I'd done that all of my life.

Even as a child, I'd refused to grieve the loss of my father. While my sister spent hours crying alone in her bedroom, I'd gone outside to play soccer. As an adult, I'd continued to hide from the pain.

So I didn't experience relief when my dad died. Instead, an emotional explosion occurred inside of me. Bottled up remorse and regret burst through my being for months. I grieved not only over my father's death but over his tragic life. He was forty-seven when he killed himself. He'd wasted so many years.

And when I'd cried all I could for him, I realized my grieving had only begun. I hadn't yet cried for myself.

One morning it began. As I sat on the couch listening to music, I finally began to cry for the six-year-old little girl who'd lost her daddy to divorce. I cried for the little girl who missed being called by her pet name, "impus-belly rupus," and who ached for her daddy's arms. I cried for the adolescent so desperate for love—and so sure she was unlovable. And I cried for what I had missed all through my life.

Big Girls Don't Cry

I had just turned twenty-three when my dad died. I'd managed to keep the anguished, hurting little girl inside of me fairly quiet for all those years. Now my dad was gone forever, and I could no longer stifle her plea: *Can I cry now?*

The mourning process takes us from loss to acceptance, from hurting to healing. But unfortunately, the saying "Big boys don't cry" can apply to girls, too. Some big girls don't cry either—even when they lose their daddy.

Mourning is often associated with death. But any major loss in our life that hurts us or takes away something we love requires mourning at some level. A child whose father dies experiences the most final kind of father-loss. However, losing Dad to divorce or abandonment is also devastating. And what about the woman who grew up with an emotionally absent, ineffective father? Her losses were subtle and daily, yet they, too, were real.

Whether your father was absent, abusive, or ineffective, the first man you ever loved let you down. And that hurt. How did you respond?

The Bible tells us there is "a time to weep and a time to laugh, a time to mourn and a time to dance" (Eccl 3:4). As a child, did you laugh when it was time to cry? Did you dance while inside a part of you died?

Barriers to Childhood Grief

Following are some common reasons why you may have postponed dealing with your grief.

Adults

Judy Tatelbaum writes in *The Courage to Grieve*, "Children's grief can easily be inhibited.... Adults can support and assist a child to grieve fully to completion, or adults can limit a child's ability to grieve by their words or injunctions and by the behavior they offer the child to imitate."[1]

How did the adults in your life treat the loss of your father?

Did they encourage you to talk about it? Did they let you cry? If not, they possibly feared evoking emotions they weren't sure how to handle. What's more, especially in the case of death, your mother, because of her own pain, might have found herself unable to reach out to her hurting daughter.

One woman wrote, "My father's death when I was ten was a wave I couldn't swim through, one that went over my head and choked me. My mother was the anchor in this tumultuous sea, a steady place for me and my two sisters and brother to hold on to. But where was her steady place? Her foundation had crumbled."[2]

Feelings of Low Self-Worth

In a room full of twenty laughing and playing children, if one is crying, who gets noticed?

To mourn is a way of validating our importance, of saying, "It matters what happened to me!" As a child, you may have felt too insignificant to lay claim to such rights. Mom deserved to cry. Others deserved to cry. But you were just another one of the kids.

Fear of Pain

To mourn is to refuse the anesthesia of ignorance and to claim our pain. Even if you felt important enough to cry, you may not have wanted to feel the hurt. To stifle and suppress the pain was easier.

Lack of Understanding

You may have failed to mourn because you didn't yet understand the enormity of your loss. If you lost your father through some means other than death, you might have assumed it was to be expected somehow. You knew you hurt, but then you quickly moved on, unaware of how profusely you were bleeding inside.

What's in a Tear?

God acknowledges the process and need for mourning throughout the Bible. We read repeatedly of people who mourned over death, unfavorable circumstances, or even their own sin. Donning sackcloth and ashes, they grieved sometimes for days on end. Today such intense grief is seldom witnessed or carried out. Does it matter?

Tears, left unshed, become stones in our hearts, weighing down our spirits. Emotional problems, depression, and suicide are linked to repressed grief. Unexpressed grief is a blanket of sadness that smothers us—one we can't identify or understand.

A harmful consequence of suppressed or unresolved grief is the inability to forgive. If we haven't allowed ourselves to experience and process the pain of father-loss, we won't come to a point of forgiveness. It is like being stuck full of arrows that we refuse to pull out and examine for fear we'll bleed to death. Our unwillingness to face the pain makes it impossible to forgive the one who shot the arrows.

So how did we ever survive? Many of us dealt with our childhood pain by covering our wounds. We wrapped them—arrows and all—in laughter. We used a possession to cover one wound; we stayed busy to cover another one. We entered adulthood resembling a swaddled mummy, unable to function under our heavy bandages.

As adults, we may have to remove the bandages that smother and numb our pain but fail to heal our hearts.

That sounds scary. We don't like to lay ourselves out naked, to feel pain. But like an arm that is broken and set wrong, God may need to break us again, that he might set our hearts right.

Stages of the Grieving Process

Mourning is a process with stages: denial, anger, bargaining, and acceptance. Many experts stress the role of guilt as well.

In my research for this book, I interviewed women at various points in their mourning of father-loss. Most women had mourned at least some. Others had never mourned their childhood losses. These women gave me a blank look when I explained the purpose and topic of my book. "So what?" they'd say. "I lost my dad. Life goes on."

Perhaps these women never moved beyond stage one: denial. They feel their father-loss hasn't affected them. Many have yet to acknowledge their own pain, much less forgive.

Other women became stuck in the anger or the blame stage and never moved on to acceptance. These became the women with a chip on their shoulders. Their anger is visible in their faces, conversations, and relationships. Mention "father" to such a woman and watch the hardness come into her eyes.

Still other daughters had experienced deep healing of their wounds. They had mourned and come to a place of forgiveness and wholeness.

If you're unsure which stage of grief you're in, that's OK. Don't try to fit yourself into a box. Rather, pray that God will reveal the next step you need to take, if any.

How Do I Mourn?

We can't force ourselves to mourn. One woman said to me, "But I don't feel anything!" That's OK. God has a time for each of us. The Holy Spirit will help us enter into a grieving process if we are willing. Reading this chapter may spark such a process. Or something else in your life may be the catalyst.

A friend who lost her father through divorce when she was six is writing a novel. As she shared her book ideas and characters with me, I said, "Karen, the orphaned little girl in your story sounds like you."

"You're right," she said. "I'm realizing that. By writing about this girl's pain, I'm sort of mourning my childhood."

Another woman, Barb, found that her grief was sparked by jealousy. She married a man with an adolescent daughter from a previous marriage. "Watching the two of them together—the way he loves and cuddles her—brings back the pain I've experienced from not having a dad."

If you've not yet grieved your losses, and you sense the Lord calling you to the graveside of your childhood, go with him.

The following steps will help you through the mourning process.

1. Remember the little girl you once were. In chapter one I wrote, "I find it hard to believe I was ever someone's little girl. If it were true, wouldn't I know it? Wouldn't I feel it?"

If you came from a father-absent or dysfunctional home, you may have blocked huge portions of your childhood memories. This was a natural defense mechanism. But to grieve your losses, you need to get in touch with that little girl. Who was she? What was she feeling? Often, if we can talk about our childhood feelings with a friend, we'll remember more than we thought.

2. Remove your bandages and look at your wounds. If your father was abusive, harsh, or neglectful, identifying your hurts is easy. They glare at you. You remember the time your father broke his promise to take you somewhere; when he called you stupid; when he hit you, hurt you, or left you alone outside the tavern. These are your father's sins of *commission*—the things he *did* against you.

What about his sins of *omission*? What about the things your dad should have done but *didn't* or *couldn't* do. Maybe he wasn't around to hurt you. But his absence hurt. The emptiness you felt at your school play when you searched the audience and saw Mom's face but not Dad's; the prick in your soul when no one was there to take you to the father-daughter tea; the lump that rose in your throat when you wondered, *Who will give me away at my wedding?*

Whether your father hurt you purposely or accidentally, your wounds exist. And you need to cry for the little girl who sustained them.

3. Be willing to feel anger. Ephesians 4:26 says, "'In your anger do not sin.' Do not let the sun go down while you are still angry."

To be angry and yet not sin means anger itself is not sinful. Even Jesus became angry. His was righteous anger, however. What made it so? His response to it. Our response to anger, not the emotion itself, is what can bring sin.

Anger becomes sin when it leads to acts or thoughts of hate, violence, or ill will. Anger also becomes sin when it leads to bitterness, which is why we are not to let the sun go down while we are still angry. God doesn't want anger to fester.

If you're afraid to grieve for fear that anger will spew out, then it must be inside of you. Perhaps the sun has set on it for years.

You were robbed of a daddy. Go ahead and release your rage. God's not afraid of your honesty or your anger.

4. Deal with false guilt. Repressed guilt, like anger, can be dangerous. Because children see the world as revolving around them, they feel responsible when Daddy leaves or dies. They wrongly assume they have caused the loss and don't feel they have the right to grieve.

As a child, Denise blamed herself for her parents' divorce. "The night before my dad left," she explains, "my brother and I got into trouble. My dad beat us. Then he said we were lucky he was leaving, and we wouldn't have to go through that again. I thought I was to blame. My brother and I begged my dad not to go. We said we'd be good; we were sorry. It didn't help, of course, and he left anyway."

101 / Can I Cry Now?

How can you recognize false guilt? *Any* guilt you feel about your father-loss is probably without basis. A child is never at fault when her father dies, leaves, or abuses her. The Holy Spirit is the one who convicts us of sin that leads to repentance, forgiveness, and release. False guilt just hangs on, nagging and whining at us.

5. Don't cry alone. "Successful" mourning takes us through intense anguish and sorrow to the other side. God helps us do this. Unless we receive comfort through the Holy Spirit, we could get stuck somewhere in a state of pain.

Matthew 5:4 says, "Blessed are those who mourn, for they will be comforted." God wants to hold you while you cry. He pats your back and says, "You're going to be all right. I understand."

You *are* valuable enough to take up God's time. And other people's! Talking with a counselor or a trusted friend can be a great way to process your feelings.

6. Don't attach a timetable. Eventually, you will no longer actively grieve your father-loss. In another sense, you may never stop. In fact, just when you think you'll never shed another tear, an older man who reminds you of your father might come along and make you cry.

Last summer my family was at the beach. We found an empty picnic table and began to put our food on it. An old man came over, leaned down, and picked up a pair of shoes from underneath the table. "Oh, I'm sorry," I said. "I didn't see those. Were you holding this table?"

"I'm waiting for my daughter," he answered. "I think she needs one, but that's okay. You can have it."

"Are you sure?" I asked.

He peered at me through his bifocals and smiled kindly. "I'm sure, honey."

What a sweet old man, I thought.

A few minutes later a middle-aged lady strolled up the beach. The old man who had given up the table went to meet her. They embraced, linked arms, and walked on down the beach. I stood entranced, watching them for more than a few moments. Before I turned back to my family, I quickly brushed my hand across my cheek.

Let your loving heavenly Father take off your old bandages and touch your wounds. Some of the wraps may resist undoing. Some of the hurts might sting. But when you're through, you'll be ready for the next chapter and the next step: forgiveness.

Time to Consider

1. Where are you in the grieving process? Where do you want to be?

2. Why is it OK for Christians to be broken and hurting? What does brokenness accomplish? What did it accomplish for David in the Psalms?

3. If you didn't mourn your father-loss as a child, what kept you from doing so? How are you dealing with that hindrance now?

4. Read Ecclesiastes 3:4. Why do people dance when they should mourn? Laugh when they should cry? How do we get on track?

5. When John relates the story of Lazarus' resurrection from the dead, he notes, "Jesus wept" (Jn 11:35). Why do you think Jesus cried when he knew Lazarus would live again?

I Want to Forgive, But ...

I never forgave my father while he was alive. Only after his death did I begin to sort through my guilt about this, as well as my feelings of guilt about his suicide. And only then could I admit I had wounds of my own that needed forgiveness. My father had hurt himself, but in the process, he'd hurt me, too. And I was angry.

My injuries weren't gaping and bleeding, but like an invisible paper cut, they stung far worse than they appeared to. Big or small, obvious or hidden, after I'd grieved the injuries and injustices surrounding my father-loss, I had a choice to make. I could hold on to them (a part of me longed to), or I could surrender them to God and forgive my father. Neither prospect appealed to me. But I had only two choices.

With Both Hands

As a baby, my oldest son, Noah, loved rattles. He would become frustrated, however, when he was clutching a rattle in each hand and then saw a third one he wanted. He'd stare at it, fuss and cry, but refuse to empty either hand in order to pick it up.

With one outstretched hand, the father-deprived daughter grasps for all that her father failed to give her. With the other hand, she clutches tightly to what her father *did* give her: her wounds.

Just as Noah refused to let go of his rattles, many women struggle with releasing their father-hurts. But until they can, they won't have a free hand to grasp forgiveness for their fathers.

Forgiveness bridges hurt and healing. As a surgeon sews up an incision so the wound can heal, forgiveness closes our wounds. When we fail to forgive, our injuries remain open, fester and burn bitterness into our souls.

We've heard plenty of sermons on forgiveness. You may be thinking, "Yeah, yeah, I know I need to forgive." But even though forgiveness is a popular topic, there still isn't enough of it to go around.

Forgiving an offense, not to mention a lifetime of offenses, is difficult even for people who understand the benefits of forgiveness. This chapter doesn't so much address why we *need* to forgive as it does why so often we *don't* forgive. What barriers keep falling across our paths as we attempt to move toward forgiving our fathers and others?

To forgive is to surrender a wound. But what if we're handing over the injury to a person we don't trust?

Careful With Those Wounds—They're Mine!

Years ago, I used to teach the four-year-old class at our church on Wednesday nights. Prayer time was a riot. The kids sat Indian-style on the floor in a crooked, wiggling circle.

"Do any of you have needs to pray for?" I asked.

Suddenly, they were earnest. Of course they did! Grabbing their feet, they rocked back and forth on their bottoms, excited for their turn to share. When at last all eyes were on an individual child, he or she proudly announced a list of latest injuries. "My knee got hurt when I fell down. My arm got scratched by my cat...."

The *worst* thing that could happen was to not have an "owie" to share. Should such misfortune occur, they would scurry to find something. Anything! Usually, they managed to produce a much-faded scar or scratch we had prayed for last week.

In the previous chapter we uncovered our emotional wounds and grieved over them. Now they are open, exposed before us. We aren't proud of them, yet we don't want them to be ignored or minimized either.

The children in our class trusted us, their teachers, to take even the least of their "owies" seriously. They knew we'd never make light of their hurt, no matter how small or old.

The father-deprived daughter, however, doesn't always trust God's reaction to her hurts. She hesitates to forgive her father and surrender her wounds for fear that God will gloss over them. She thinks her injuries matter to God only so far as she forgives the one who hurt her.

Imagine you are a child on the playground, and a bully has brutally beaten you. Your nose is bleeding; your arms and legs are raw. You cry out, "Teacher, did you see that? He beat me up—for no reason."

The teacher walks over. "Of course I saw. But all that matters now is that you forgive the bully!" She takes the bully by the hand and says, "Even if this girl can't forgive you, I do!" She walks away with him, leaving you dazed, hurting, still sprawled on the playground cement.

This is how some of us perceive God's approach—and certain people's approach—to forgiveness. Something inside rises up in protest. *Does no one care about what happened to me?*

In Search of a Champion

Recently a friend, Carol, discovered that her husband was in love with another woman, whom I'll call Jennifer. Carol told me she'd called another friend for prayer.

"I don't understand it," she said. "But what helped me the most was when my friend prayed about 'this Jennifer chick, Lord.' She called her that a couple times and for some reason, that meant so much to me."

Why did this seemingly small act, the way her friend referred to the "other" woman in prayer, help Carol so much? Because this friend voiced anger against the woman who was seducing Carol's husband.

The *American Heritage Dictionary* defines a champion as "one that defends, fights for or supports a cause or another person." Carol needed a champion, and her friend not only took on that role but approached God in a way that implied he, too, was Carol's champion.

Many father-deprived daughters with deep wounds are unable to let go of them because they don't see God as their champion. They don't think he is at all angry about how their fathers hurt them. Instead, when God asks them to forgive, they imagine him saying, "Yes, your dad hurt you. But it doesn't really matter now. Let's pretend it never happened."

No wonder the little girl inside clutches more tightly to her wounds. She hasn't felt valuable all her life, and now she can't bear to have her injuries count for nothing.

God doesn't respond to us this way. He *is* our champion. He cares deeply about what has happened to us. Why do we doubt that?

Most of us are familiar with God's forgiving nature. Nehemiah 9:17 says, "You are a forgiving God, gracious and compassionate, slow to anger and abounding in love." We know that "there is now no condemnation for those who are in Christ Jesus" (Rom 8:1).

Problems arise, however, if we think that God's forgiveness and mercy eradicate his role as Judge.

J.I. Packer points out in *Knowing God*, "There are few things stressed more strongly in the Bible than the reality of God's work as Judge."[1] Many of us hesitate to ascribe the role of judge to God. Perhaps we confuse judgment with condemnation. A new building is judged to see whether it meets building code requirements. An old building that is condemned, however, is mercilessly demolished.

We cannot see God as our champion if we don't believe he is still a holy God, a God who gets angry about sin and who "will 'give to each person according to what he has done'" (Rom 2:6).

My point is not that we should delight in any judgment our fathers or others might undergo. That's not forgiveness. But we must know God as both a forgiver and a judge in order to fully understand that he is our champion. We can surrender our wounds to him because he will take them seriously. We can offer forgiveness to our fathers because we have a God who cares.

King David knew God as both a judge and champion. He declared, "My shield is God Most High, who saves the upright in heart. God is a righteous judge, a God who expresses his wrath every day" (Ps 7:10, 11).

David was sure that God was his champion and so could forgive his enemies, even sparing Saul's life after Saul had repeatedly tried to kill him. (See 1 Samuel 24:1-7.)

Peter tells us to imitate Jesus' attitude: "When they hurled their insults at him, he did not retaliate; when he suffered, he made no threats. Instead, he entrusted himself to him who judges justly" (1 Pt 2:23).

God cares about your pain. As you forgive your father, God will join you. As you release the resentment toward your father over the past, God will not gloss over your wounds or take them lightly. He is your champion.

111 / I Want to Forgive, But ...

Other Barriers to Forgiveness

Inability to trust God with our wounds is one of many barriers that blocks forgiveness. But these are some others:

Unresolved Grief

The last chapter discussed how failure to mourn our losses prevents forgiveness. We stand across from our fathers and say, "You might have hit me. But it didn't hurt. I didn't feel it." When we deny our pain and refuse to deal with an offense, we can't forgive.

Jesus not only acknowledged our offenses, "he himself bore our sins in his body on the tree, so that we might die to sins and live for righteousness" (1 Pt 2:24). If he had simply ignored our sins, Jesus couldn't have overcome and forgiven them.

Misconceptions

Despite teachings on forgiveness, false philosophies still flourish. Two common misconceptions about forgiveness involve feelings and forgetting.

The first is, "I can't forgive because I still *feel* angry." Someone has injured you. Your heart isn't overflowing with warm sensations for this person, and you conclude that to forgive would be a farce.

But Jesus didn't ask us to *feel* like forgiving, only to *choose* to forgive. Jesus didn't *feel* like going to the cross. He labored and agonized over it. Ultimately, he prayed, "Not my will, but yours be done" (Lk 22:42).

A second misconception is, "I can't forgive because I can't forget." But nowhere in the Bible are we told to "forgive and forget." God in his omnipotence "remembers your sins no more" (Is 43:25). But we're human and can't obliterate an incident from our minds.

It's true that we should not keep reminding the offender of the mistake, but if we forgive and our wounds are healed, we should be able to gaze upon the offender once again. Our scars become a testimony to God's grace and power.

Rebellion

Ephesians 4:32 says, "Be kind and compassionate to one another, forgiving each other, just as in Christ God forgave you."

Our old sin nature hangs on for dear life, resisting the idea of forgiveness. But God's intention is always for our good. He knows that bitterness and unforgiveness will infect our lives and the lives of others with pain.

Fear of Failure

I once loved credit cards. Plastic was fantastic—until the bill arrived and I couldn't afford the payments. Likewise, you may fear that you can't afford to forgive all the wrongs done against you. You've got father-hurts valued at ten thousand dollars and a measly ten dollars worth of mercy to cover them. You're afraid to attempt to forgive in case you come up short. Why try?

But wait! Someone rich in mercy waits to come to your rescue and make up the difference. We can charge these debts, the wounds from our fathers, to his account. The Bible tells us that God is "rich in mercy" (Eph 2:4), and that he "defends the cause of the fatherless" (Dt 10:18).

But how can God supply forgiveness for sins and injuries not against him? Because in a sense, they *are* against him. Jesus makes it clear in the parable of the goats and the sheep in Matthew 25:31-45 that when we neglect or oppress others, it is as if we are doing these things to him.

Remember that Christmas Eve when your father came home in a drunken stupor and slapped you because you asked about toys? Jesus felt the force of that hand across his cheek, too. Remember when your dad hugged you close, told you he loved you, and then walked out of your life forever? Jesus also watched him disappear.

Do you believe God was with you every minute of your childhood? He, even more than you, knows the nature of the crimes against you. As you attempt to forgive, the Holy Spirit can make up for your deficiencies. The debts you've forgiven will never come back marked "insufficient funds."

There They Are, Lord!

I remember once when I took my two boys to the park, where Nathan got into a squabble with another child. He ran to me and cried, "Mom, look! See that boy on the monkey bars with the motorcycle on his shirt? He hit me!"

Nathan expected me to care about who had mistreated him. And I did. In the same way, God cares about who hurt you.

Go to him and point out each person, one by one.

Your dad is first. Can you surrender your wounds to God, your champion, and forgive your father?

And Mom. Do you need to forgive her too?

What about your siblings? I had to ask my sister's forgiveness for how I treated her while we were growing up. I screamed hateful words at her, ripped up her religious posters, and physically attacked her. She has forgiven me. What freedom! Do you need to forgive a brother or sister who hurt you?

If you had a stepfather, can you forgive him for failing to fill the role of daddy? Or do you need to forgive him for making a miserable mess of an already messy situation?

What about teachers, friends, and others? Whom do you link with a hurt or pain? Don't spend hours pondering this. Just ask God to bring people to mind, and then allow the Holy Spirit to dig deeply.

Two Types of Forgiveness

Forgiveness is a sensitive subject in psychological circles today. One concern is that people suppress their rage and anger, and use forgiveness to prematurely close the loop of healing.

For this reason, I placed the chapter "Can I Cry Now?" prior to this one. We must release some of the anger and grief before trying to forgive. But note author Rita Bennett's words about two kinds of forgiveness.

"How can you forgive right away, and yet take time to get in touch with your deep feelings?" she writes. "You can forgive *with your will* immediately, or at least by the end of the day, and then forgive deeply *with your emotions* from the past, taking time to do this, perhaps over a period of years."[2]

If you choose to forgive your father today, even though you don't *feel* you can, God will honor your obedience. Whether you've forgiven with your will or your emotions, you can do two simple things to give your forgiveness strong roots.

First, if you are already in an active relationship with your father, deliver your forgiveness in person. This will nail it down more firmly for you and him. Could you write a letter or make a phone call explaining your decision to forgive?

If you haven't been speaking with your father, you may want to let your forgiveness have time to settle in your own heart for a while. You may also want to reestablish conversation with your father before you communicate your forgiveness.

Maybe, as in my case, your dad is no longer alive. I resolved my dilemma by asking God to tell my father (I believe he's in heaven) that I've forgiven him. I have no scriptural basis for this, but I don't see it conflicting with the Bible and it has helped me.

Second, pray for your father. Matthew 5:44 says, "But I tell you: Love your enemies and pray for those who persecute you." As you pray, you will begin to see him through Christ's eyes—and catch some of Christ's contagious compassion.

Some fathers have committed acts that are unforgivable. But God's grace is greater than their sin. With God's help as your champion, you can forgive your father.

As we'll see in the next chapter, sometimes we have to forgive again and again. You've opened your hand and surrendered your father-wounds. But what if your dad is still hurting you today?

Time to Consider

1. Which of the barriers to forgiveness mentioned in this chapter have you encountered? How have you dealt with them?

2. Which of your father-hurts do you find hardest to forgive? Which of them is your fist still tightly clutched around and why? What will you do to release these?

3. Have you experienced God as your champion? If so, how? If not, what do you think is the hindrance? How do you feel about God as a judge?

4. Who, if anyone, do you need to forgive for past hurts? How will that affect your relationship with that person?

5. If you have decided to forgive your father, how will you communicate that to him? If you can't tell him in person, what will you do?

t e n

What Now, Dad?

*T*he funeral service for my father, James Hilliard Lloyd, took place at a funeral home in Salem, Oregon. My siblings and their spouses attended, as well as some of my dad's friends from the halfway house where he'd stayed.

In a small side room, my father's body was available for viewing. After the service, my sister and I went in to see him. He was dressed in a tacky brown polyester suit with an emerald-green tie. For several moments we stood silently staring at him, saying nothing. I longed to bid him an emotional farewell like I'd seen in the movies, but I couldn't.

When it was time to go, Kathy finally said, "We love you, Dad. Good-bye." I was thankful she'd voiced the words for both of us. But I wasn't ready to leave. I hesitated in the doorway, gripping the door frame with my hand. How could I walk out of that room, knowing I would never see my dad again? Certainly my heart would lock up and freeze if I even tried to let go.

During the last five years of my dad's life, I vacillated between hope and despair, clinging to the possibility that someday he'd get well. I wanted this for him. But I also wanted it for me. I wanted him to recover so that he could become the father I needed.

To leave that room and my father behind was to accept defeat forever, to say good-bye to the daddy that never was—and now, could never be.

Ties That Bind

Forcing my legs to carry me away from my dead father was painful. But holding on to him while he was alive had hurt even more. As long as I was waiting for my father to become what he couldn't, I was disappointed. Holding on made it impossible to move forward with my life or find healing for my wounds.

Hopefully, you've grieved the loss of your father and forgiven him for the injuries he inflicted in the past. But what about today? Many women are still experiencing the loss of their fathers even as adults. They ask, "How can I get healed when I keep getting hurt?"

We've seen how the father-deprived daughter searches in many places for all her father failed to give her. But did she ever really give up the idea that Daddy himself might still come through? Did she let go of him? Or did she stay tied to him despite the pain?

The latter is most often the case. Adult daughters stay painfully connected to their fathers for a variety of reasons and in a variety of ways. Some women are waiting for their fathers to change, as I was. Some daughters are chasing dads that won't be caught. Others can't let their dead fathers die.

You can't overcome the consequences of father-loss and

begin to take responsibility for your life if you are still in the process of losing your father. And you cannot get healed while you are still getting hurt. Like a kite caught in a high tree and entangled in string that must be cut free, you too must cut the ties that bind you to your father in a hurtful way.

To close the wounds of father-loss and move forward with our lives, we must emotionally *leave* our fathers.

The Disappointed Daughter

Perhaps your father is living a destructive lifestyle, or for some other reason his behavior continues to disappoint you. For years you've waited for him to change. To hope or pray for your dad isn't wrong. But beware of clinging expectations.

Expectations are like yo-yos. You may think you've released your dad, but the string remains tied around your finger. And every time your dad disappoints you, it yanks you down hard. Each time my dad dropped out of a treatment program or failed to take the steps toward recovery, I became frustrated and hurt all over again.

Some years ago, Dr. James Dobson published an excerpt from a letter he wrote to a woman whose father continually disappointed her.

"Your dad never met the needs that a father should satisfy in his little girl, and I think you are still hoping he will miraculously become what he has never been. Therefore, he constantly disappoints you—hurts you—rejects you. I think you will be less vulnerable to pain when you accept the fact that he cannot, nor will he ever, provide the love and empathy and interest that he should.... *It hurts less to expect nothing than to hope in vain*" (italics added).[1]

Can you release your father from your expectations? Can you cut that string?

If your father continues to live a self-destructive or abusive lifestyle, you might need to determine whether you're playing an enabling role. Naturally, we want to give of ourselves unselfishly to our fathers. But a point comes when well-intentioned giving can contribute to an unhealthy cycle of behavior.

The Rejected Daughter

Some fathers totally reject their young daughters. These daughters are devastated when, as adults, they continue to search for some sign of acceptance or love and find nothing.

Cindy's father cut himself off from her when she was ten. He has refused to see or talk to her since. She found out his phone number and calls his answering machine just to hear the sound of his voice. *Ouch.*

Daughters like Cindy whose fathers have completely rejected them don't appear connected to their fathers at all. But a closer look often reveals their bonds.

In the famous gold rush of 1849, thousands of people descended on California in search of gold. Some discovered it. But many people didn't. They wasted months, even years, of their lives enduring poverty, hunger, sickness, and cold. In spite of the painfully high price of their quest, they couldn't give up the search and go home.

To be rejected by one's father is painful enough. But to stop searching for his acceptance is to experience the full impact of his rejection. For this reason, many daughters subconsciously refuse to give up hope that someday their fathers will rouse themselves from their comas of apathy, run to them, scoop them up, and say, "How could I have ever let you go?"

My sister-in-law, Tami, lost her father through divorce at age eleven. She's seen him only once since then. Meanwhile, she's faithfully sent him cards, letters, a wedding invitation, birth announcements of her children—and received no response.

Should Tami and others like her give up hope?

Yes and no. Many daughters stand in the river bed searching for the gold of acceptance for too long. They are cold, tired, and shaking. Meanwhile, their wounds stay wet; they can't heal. If a daughter's back aches from bending over, if her father keeps offering her jagged rocks instead of gems, she might as well get out of the water. She must accept the fact that she may never find father-love in this particular river.

Understand here that while you may need to accept rejection, and to let go, your father is really demonstrating his *own* emotional handicaps, his *own* inability to love. He's probably not *able* to offer you the love and acceptance you need. Remembering that will empower you to climb out of the river bed, dry off, go home, and move forward with your life.

The Regretful Daughter

As a child, I loved Shirley Temple. Her movie, "The Little Princess," especially struck a chord with me. She plays a girl named Sarah who is told that her father is dead, killed in a war. She refuses to believe it and presses on relentlessly trying to find him. Finally, toward the end of the movie, she stumbles into a room where she finds her father, bandaged, in a wheelchair, but alive!

She runs to him and hugs him, "Daddy, Daddy!"

Due to his illness, her father doesn't recognize her at first. Then, as she sobs into his chest, begging him to know her, he does. "Sarah! Sarah! My little girl!"

Their reunion is blissful.

Unfortunately, life is not like the movies. Daughters whose fathers have died won't stumble into a room and find them alive.

This, however, doesn't mean they can easily let go of their fathers. A daughter often tries to keep her dead father alive by clinging to regrets and "if only's." She dwells on what she should've done or said but didn't. She thinks about what life would be like if her father hadn't died and imagines how he might have made things better for her—or vice versa.

Dr. Norm Wright suggests that a woman with regrets make a detailed list of them. She can then read them aloud either to an empty chair or a trusted friend or counselor. "Be compassionate toward yourself as you complete the exercise," he says.

"It may help to remember that you probably aren't the only person in your father-daughter relationship who has regrets," he writes. "Your father undoubtedly carries—or carried to his grave—his own list of regrets. Very few of us say or do all that we intend or wish we had done. That's why we must be thankful for the gift of forgiveness that God has given us for ourselves and others."[2]

If you are still unable to let go of your dead father, maybe you haven't completed your mourning process. Acceptance and release are the final stages.

Eventually, you will need to close the door to the room into which you stumbled, hoping to find your father alive. I know how much that hurts. But refusal to accept the fact that you're never going to find your father alive in that room hurts more. It's time to say good-bye.

The Estranged Daughter

Many fathers who abused or deeply hurt their daughters are estranged from them today. These daughters aren't searching for acceptance or holding on to expectations. But they remain connected to their fathers through unresolved relationships.

Marla, thirty-two, has refused to speak to her father for three years. On the surface she appears angry and at times even apathetic. But the little girl inside of her can't put her relationship with her father to rest. Cut off at a painful point, the relationship hangs open, unfinished inside her heart.

Hebrews 12:1 says, "Let us throw off everything that hinders and the sin that so easily entangles, and let us run with perseverance the race marked out for us."

The estranged daughter tries to run her race, but she keeps stepping on the shattered pieces of the broken relationship with her father. Cutting herself off from him didn't stop the hurting, and inside she knows the door was shut before the conflict was fully played out. She must face her father once again.

Confronting Daddy

Are you emotionally or physically estranged from your father? Does he continue to mistreat you today? You may want to consider confronting him.

A confrontation is an attempt to make peace with your father "if it is possible, as far as it depends on you" (Rom 12:18). It may mean opening up a slammed door, although you might not enter back into an *active* relationship with your dad. It is also an opportunity to express feelings you may have kept repressed for years.

The purpose of a confrontation is not to spew hate or anger but to speak the truth in love (see Ephesians 4:15); to give your father a chance to account for his behavior.

Set up a specific time to meet with your dad and plan ahead what you want to say. How did he hurt you? How did that make you feel? How is he still hurting you?

Be prepared for resistance or defensiveness, and try to confront with the purpose of forgiveness and release. Examine your own heart. Did you sin in your response to your father's failures? Do you need to ask his forgiveness? If so, this is a great starting place for a confrontation.

If your father is dead, you can confront him in a letter. A letter is also appropriate if your dad lives far away or if you're unable to speak the words face-to-face.

However you decide to confront, try to release all unrealistic expectations about what it will accomplish.

Remember Diane who became promiscuous and whose father didn't seem to care? Several years ago, she asked his forgiveness for her own behavior growing up. She didn't expect him to reciprocate, but he did. "In fact," she says, "he said everything I'd ever wanted to hear. That he was sorry, that our family's pain had been his fault, that I'd acted the way I did because of him. This helped me let go of my resentments and accept him and myself more. But it didn't change him. He is still distant and uncaring."

Diane's story illustrates that even a "successful" confrontation may not change a father's behavior.

Free to Honor

As we surrender our expectations of dysfunctional fathers, say good-bye to dead fathers, resolve relationships with estranged fathers, and abandon the painful search for acceptance, we'll be free to honor our fathers.

Father-deprived daughters have a difficult time with the Scripture, "'Honor your father and mother'—which is the first commandment with a promise—'that it may go well with you and that you may enjoy long life on the earth'" (Eph 6:2, 3).

Isn't God asking a lot, that we honor these dads who did

little to earn our respect? But God knows that if we are not honoring them, we are searching for them, blaming them, or resenting them. Honoring our fathers is for our benefit, "that it might go well" with us.

To honor your dad, must you pretend your father's failures or shortcomings don't exist? No. To honor is to purpose to esteem and respect our dads *despite their shortcomings.* We communicate honor by our tone of voice, our words, and our response to someone—even when that person isn't present. Even if your father is dead, you can choose to honor his memory.

If you find it difficult to honor your father, try to honor him "as unto the Lord." When you honor your father out of obedience, you honor God. And he is worthy.

Another Room, Another River, Another Father

Cutting unhealthy connections to our fathers and letting go of them is a painful process. But the good news is that you don't have to totally abandon the search for a father. You need only redirect it. Once you stop looking where it hurts too much to look, you'll be free to put your hope where it will not disappoint.

Our heavenly Father has a throne room where all his children are welcomed, recognized, and rejoiced over. You can always find him there. From his throne room flows a river of life, a river rich with the gold of father-love.

No matter what happens with our earthly fathers in years to

come—though we are rejected, ignored, abused, forgotten—
we have another Father who will not destroy our hope in him.
A Father some of you have yet to meet as *Abba*, though you
may know him already as Lord.

Time to Consider

1. If your father is alive, in what ways are you still holding on
   to him or searching for him? What steps can you take to let
   go?

2. If your father has passed away, to what regrets or "if only's"
   do you cling? What can you do about this block to healing?

3. If you decide to confront your father, what do you want to
   communicate to him? How do you think he will respond?
   How will you respond in turn?

4. Specifically, how could you show your father you honor
   him?

5. How will honoring your father make him feel? How will it
   make you feel?

I Have Another Father

*A*bout a year after our father died, my sister Kathy became suicidal and was admitted into the psychiatric ward of the hospital. She had attempted suicide in the past. Now her despair was an unprotested submission to defeat. Five years of counseling and prayer seemed to have changed little inside of her.

While in the hospital, she refused to see visitors and expressed little interest in returning home to her husband and two children. Her doctor released her ten days later, but she continued to speak of defeat. "I'm so tired of trying," she told me one day. "I don't feel close to God. I don't care about living. If it weren't for my kids, I'd just give up."

I love my sister in a way that defies words. When she said these things, I felt afraid for her and for myself. I'd lost my father; would I lose her, too?

The situation stung with irony. My sister was first to accept Jesus as her Savior; she eventually led all of her siblings to the Lord. Her stubborn love for me convinced me of the reality of God. Now she could not seem to find him.

My thoughts flew back to the Father's Day just a few weeks after my dad's suicide. Kathy and I had gone into a card shop and found ourselves picking through the Father's Day cards. The mushy and glowing tributes struck us as ludicrous. Did such a father exist?

We'd stood in the middle of the store and laughed so hard we cried—or was it the other way around?

Distorted Images

Kathy had entered into a relationship with God thirteen years before her hospitalization at age twenty-seven. But knowing God didn't keep her from hurting, becoming depressed, and considering suicide. Why?

The question is not whether God failed my sister or my sister failed God. Rather, what kind of God did Kathy know? Better yet, what kind of Father did she imagine God to be? Did she know a Father God who appreciated the smallest things about her and thought she was special? Or did she imagine a God who preferred more "together" Christians? Did she know a Father God who loved to spend time with her? Or did she imagine a God who would get on a train and leave her behind?

As a child you were probably taught that God was the biggest boss of all. Even grown-ups were supposed to "mind" him. And while you couldn't actually see God, your own father modeled him for you, accurately or not.

Perhaps you attended church and were told God was good. But if your father was absent or ineffective, you ran into the same problem as my sister. You couldn't reconcile a positive image of God with the distorted picture your father presented. This warped image of God hid the very thing for which you searched.

If you have finally let go of your father, you are free to find another Father in God. However, has your subconscious painted a picture of God for you that has disqualified him for that role?

What Color God Did You Paint?

Imagine that you were given a blank canvas at birth. Your father's words and actions (or lack thereof) provided the tools, paints, and brushes, with which you could paint an image of God as you grew up. What color God did you paint?

If your father was absent, due to divorce or abandonment, you were left with a blank canvas and only a few tools. Perhaps you didn't even believe in the existence of God. You had no reason to believe in a loving earthly father, much less a heavenly one.

On the other hand, an absent father may have worked to your advantage.

Remember Shelly, who was angry with her music teachers? Her mother never remarried. She says, "I got my ideas about Daddy from other places, TV shows like *Father Knows Best.* I always imagined if I'd had a dad, he'd be like that—strong, caring, supportive. When I came to know God, it was easy to think of him as a loving Father. I welcomed the idea."

Daughters who don't have to fight negative father images

are sometimes more receptive to a fatherlike God. Most of you, however, experienced some interaction with your father that left you negatively predisposed toward God.

If your father was emotionally distant and unattainable, you may have painted a picture of a God who was hard to find in times of need. You were provided with pastel paints, barely visible whites and pale pinks. You were unsure of God's care for you and imagined that he deliberately removed himself from you.

If your father was ineffective because of a problem such as alcoholism, he may have provided you with a variety of paints, but depicted a God who was a mass of contradictions. Your canvas resembled a kindergarten finger painting: splatters of confusion, swirls of doubt. You never knew what to expect from God.

The abusive, harsh, or domineering father usually does the most damage. If you would describe your dad this way, your canvas was probably covered with dark, foreboding colors. Blacks and browns. You painted a God who was angry, volatile, and demanding. You couldn't please him no matter how hard you tried.

These images of God you drew as a child were upsetting. As you grew older you tried to throw a tarp over these paintings of a God who was like your father. But still the canvas existed, coloring your thoughts and attitudes about God. When and if you met him on a personal level, you probably wanted to avoid the concept of God as a Father. So you focused on Jesus.

Fixing Our Eyes on Jesus

Many father-deprived daughters cling to the person of Jesus to crowd out negative ideas about a God who might be like their fathers. Jesus came and died for them; Jesus was the Son, not the Father. As Savior, he seems more approachable. To relate intimately with Jesus is wonderful. Hebrews 12:2 tells us to "fix our eyes on Jesus, the author and perfecter of our faith."

However, when we fix our eyes on Jesus so that we can't see God the Father, that is, when we identify *only* with Jesus, we are not really seeing Jesus at all. For Jesus points to and reveals God as Father. Jesus died as a sacrifice for sin and was raised from the dead, but he also came to revolutionize forever our view of God.

God has never changed. (See Hebrews 13:8.) Even though Jesus more fully revealed God as Father, he was our Father from the beginning. The Old Testament prophet Isaiah declared, "O Lord, you are our Father" (Is 64:8). King David rightly discerned, "As a father has compassion on his children, so the Lord has compassion on those who fear him" (Ps 103:13).

Although God hasn't changed, our covenant with him changed when Jesus came. Jesus became the way to God. "I am the way and the truth and the life. No one comes to the Father except through me" (Jn 14:6). Throughout the Gospels, Jesus attempts to reveal the loving fatherhood of God and bring people to him.

Notice how Jesus addressed God. Time and again Jesus

referred to him as Father. And not only as Father but as *Abba*, an Aramaic word meaning "daddy" or "papa" (Mk 14:36).

Jesus called God his Father in his first recorded words. When Mary and Joseph became separated from him and then found him in the temple, he said to them, "Didn't you know I had to be in my Father's house?" (Lk 2:49).

Of course, Jesus was God's Son, born of the Virgin Mary. However, he did not call God his Father only for this reason. If so, he wouldn't have taught his followers to do likewise, saying, "This, then, is how you should pray: 'Our Father in heaven ...'" (Mt 6:9).

In Jesus' time, it was scandalous for anyone to call God his Father. For hundreds of years, Jews had gone to great lengths to avoid even using God's proper name, *Yahweh*. They used the passive voice to avoid referring to God's name at all, out of reverence.

Jesus also taught that not only does God want us to address him as Father, he wants us to relate to him as a child to a parent. "Unless you change and become like little children, you will never enter the kingdom of heaven" (Mt 18:3).

Jesus emphasized that God was our perfect Father, better than any earthly father. "If you, then, though you are evil, know how to give good gifts to your children, how much more will your Father in heaven give good gifts to those who ask him!" (Mt 7:11).

Perhaps Jesus' greatest testimony to the fatherhood of God was his own behavior. When we read of him in Scripture, we can take comfort in his loving manner, his sacrificial life, and the way he took the children into his arms. But when Jesus did these things, God the Father did them, as well. Jesus is God. "Anyone who has seen me has seen the Father" (Jn 14:9). "I do exactly what my Father has commanded me" (Jn 14:31).

All Jesus' character traits are those of God himself. Through Jesus' words and actions, God endeavored to draw us closer to himself. Take a second look. As you fix your eyes on Jesus, what do you see? Do you see him pointing the way to a loving, caring Father who is anxious for his children to know his love?

Prodigal Daughters

You probably don't think of yourself as a prodigal daughter. The word "prodigal" conjures up images of waywardness or abandonment of your relationship with God. It can mean that. However, you can experience a relationship with the Lord and still make the same mistakes as the prodigal son.

The story is found in Luke 15:11-32. The son is anxious to venture out on his own. He takes his inheritance and leaves his father's house. He squanders his money and finds a job feeding pigs. When he becomes hungry enough to eat pig food, he says, "How many of my father's hired men have food to spare, and here I am starving to death!" (Lk 15:17).

He decides to head home and plead for mercy. Maybe his father will hire him. "But while he was still a long way off, his father saw him and was filled with compassion for him; he ran to his son, threw his arms around him and kissed him" (v. 20). Then his dad threw him a welcoming home party.

An important point of this story is that our Father God will always accept us back when we've sinned and gone astray. But just as important is the prodigal son's point of view. He made a mistake by leaving. He was foolish to spend all of his money. *But the gravest error he made was to doubt his father.* He thought he knew his dad. He'd lived his whole life with his father, but did he really know him?

My sister knew God when she became so despondent and wanted to take her life. But did she know him as her Father?

What if the prodigal son had so mistaken his father that he'd never gone home and discovered that his dad's love knew no bounds? Where would his despair have taken him?

Preparing to Repaint

Our failing or absent fathers determined how the paints splashed onto our canvases. The paint dried long ago, and for many of us, our canvas has remained unchanged, the image upon it unchallenged—until today.

In the next chapter, we will repaint those canvases. What kind of God will you paint? Will he remain a distant unattainable Father, available only philosophically? Or will you repaint God with such true colors that he becomes Daddy, your *Abba* Father?

You'll have to decide where to paint yourself in relationship to God. Will you stand outside of his throne room, afraid to enter? Or will you paint yourself on his lap? How old will you be? Too old for hugs and love? Too old to be desperate for a daddy?

I recently overheard a woman talking on a pay phone. I assumed by her smile, manner, and intimate tone of voice that she was speaking to her husband or boyfriend. But before she hung up I heard her say, "Bye-bye, Daddy."

I was incredulous. This woman was at least thirty-five years old. Never had I heard a grown woman address her father as "Daddy." When I asked her about it, she smiled and explained, "It's been that way with us all my life. We're close. He's one of my best friends. He's always been Daddy, and I guess he always will be."

This woman can call her father Daddy because she has experienced that kind of relationship with him. You may all but choke on the term.

A daddy is available, huggable, and strong. He doesn't divorce your mom, die in a car wreck, drink too much alcohol, abuse or neglect you. The word "daddy" probably never became real to you. As such, it sums up everything you've lost—and all you're searching for.

Right now, God is probably not your Daddy. He is, at most, your heavenly Father, a far-off, distant, unattainable God.

Before you can end your search for a father, before you can call God Daddy, you must experience the kind of relationship that this woman on the phone had with her father. You need to feel the amazement the prodigal son must have felt. You need to encounter God on the road. You need a revelation. But how?

God has given us the Holy Spirit, who is able to call what is not into being. But we must ask him. Romans 8:15 says, "For you did not receive a spirit that makes you a slave again to fear,

but you received the Spirit of sonship [daughtership]. And by
him we cry, '*Abba*, Father.'"

Can you allow God to wipe away the old picture on your
canvas? Can you cry out to him for a revelation of his father-
love for you?

After my sister was released from the hospital, I wrote her a
poem. I know now that this poem was not only for Kathy but
for all of my sisters who need another Father.

"Another Father"

Sister,
it's Father's Day.
You and I stand in the card shop,
laughing.
"Thanks, Dad, for being so wonderful."
We read aloud towering tributes
to fathers who care,
fathers who were always there.
I think I see you crying;
people are starting to stare.
The words are painfully funny—
especially now,
now that he's chosen
to become ashes.
Do you still hurt?
I know I do.
But the tears are edged with joy,
for we have found another father
who will not destroy

our hope in him.
Though strong knees were absent,
his arms now enfold
our hearts with tender care.
Though the little girl's love
roamed, lost, unclaimed,
she will never be abandoned again.
Sister,
don't forget
to let him touch you today.

Time to Consider

1. What kind of God did you paint while growing up? How are these attributes connected to your father-loss? How is God changing your painting now?

2. Which part of your canvas will you have the most difficulty painting over? Why?

3. In what ways are you a prodigal daughter still "a long way off"?

4. Today when you pray, how do you address God? How do you feel God responds to you?

5. Are you willing to find another Father? How will you seek him?

I Can Say *Abba*

*T*he same week my sister Kathy received my poem in the mail, she met her *Abba* Father for the first time.

She had awakened with a heavy heart that morning, but nevertheless made a halfhearted attempt at prayer. Suddenly, something happened inside her spirit. She felt God pour his overwhelming love into her. She'd never experienced love like that before, love strong enough to touch the deepest parts of her.

She began to cry. She saw herself as a small child, about six or seven. Jesus was there and lifted her up onto God's lap. She was a little scared, but she knew Jesus wanted her to be there.

God lifted her chin and looked into her face. He said he loved her, that she was priceless and special, his very own daughter. She was on his lap for a long time, crying into his chest and letting him love her.

In her "revelation" Kathy saw herself wearing a navy coat with orange trim. Later she asked our mother if she'd ever owned such a coat. Mom produced a photograph of Kathy at about age seven, wearing a navy coat with orange trim.

For the first time in her life, she knew God really wanted to be her Father and that he loved her as his daughter.

The Road to *Abba* Father

Kathy continues to fight depression on occasion and struggles with low self-esteem. Her "revelation" was not the end of her problems but the beginning of hope. Life will never be the same for my sister now that she's found a Father in God.

The rest of us may never have a vivid experience as Kathy did. My own revelation that God is my Father, my Daddy, has come slowly, bit by bit.

In your search for a father, the time will come when you too can finally see God's lap. But how do you get up there?

Remember the road to Oz? Dorothy and her friends finally reached the wizard, only to be terrified. They had to perform a difficult feat to receive what they were seeking. They left Oz with heavy hearts.

Jesus has traveled the road to *Abba* Father before you. God will not send you away to earn what you seek. He is expecting you and will welcome you with open arms.

"For we do not have a high priest who is unable to sympathize with our weaknesses, but we have one who has been tempted in every way, just as we are—yet was without sin. Let us then approach the throne of grace with confidence, so that we may receive mercy and find grace to help us in our time of need" (Heb 4:15, 16). We can boldly approach *Abba* Father because Jesus has opened up the way.

And yet, any relationship takes two. If God is to become Father, we have a responsibility and so does he. Get your paintbrush ready because we're about to discuss God's part. What kind of a father is God? What will happen when you climb up on his lap?

God's Part: The Faithful Father

What makes a good father? Whatever it is, God has it in abundance. If you're ever in doubt about God's response to you in a given situation, ask yourself: What would a perfect father do?

The two most important things a father gives his child are love and discipline. The two are entwined, each making the other more meaningful. The lack of, or warping of, these two necessities hurts us most as children.

It is that little girl inside of us that needs to have a relationship with *Abba* Father. Only he can restore what was lost in our childhood. Only he can provide the needed love and discipline that will cause that little girl to grow into maturity and to stop seeking a daddy in the wrong places.

How does God handle the fundamentals of discipline and love?

Abba Father's Discipline

I remember one time prior to my parents' divorce when my father disciplined me. Back then, he had a large, dignified-looking den. I was in deep trouble if he took me there to discipline me.

This particular night I received a harsh spanking from my father in his den. It hurt. I wailed. And I felt sincerely sorry for my mischief.

I was shocked when after a few minutes, my dad went to a drawer, pulled out a candy bar, and gave it to me. This is one of the few fond memories I have of him and myself as a child.

I hadn't thought about this incident for many years until recently when I got in trouble with God. I had committed an on-purpose-and-you-know-better kind of sin. I'd received a "spiritual spanking" of sorts in God's den, and I'd grieved my mistake.

It hurts sometimes to allow God to deal with me as my Father in this way. But I need to be dealt with firmly so that I don't sin again. And I know that after I have repented and have cried for a little while, he will comfort me. He will offer a candy bar.

The father-deprived daughter shudders at the idea of God's discipline. She may have no fond memories of candy bars in dens. She imagines that God's discipline is like the fallible, earthly discipline she experienced growing up.

Let's look more closely at what makes God's den a good place:

1. God's discipline proves we are his much-loved children. Many of you grew up without proper guidelines and boundaries. For a time, you enjoyed the freedom. But in the end, lack of discipline produced heartache, bondage to sin, and an inner conviction that you weren't important.

In contrast, Hebrews 12:6 says, "The Lord disciplines those he loves, and he punishes everyone he accepts as a son [daughter]."

I remind my kids more often than they like to hear that I discipline them because I care. God does, too.

2. God's discipline is perfectly motivated. When and if your father disciplined you, his motives were sometimes flawed. Anger or selfishness may have prompted his actions. No wonder his discipline hurt rather than helped.

Hebrews 12:10 says, "Our fathers disciplined us for a little while as they thought best; but God disciplines us *for our good*, that we may share in his holiness" (italics added).

Our fathers' motives were fallible. God's motive is always love and for our best.

3. God's discipline works. How did you respond to discipline as you grew up? Did it make you feel angry and rebellious?

God's discipline consists of guidelines given in Scripture, the conviction of the Holy Spirit, and the natural consequences of sin. God makes the rules clear, lets us reap what we sow, and then looks searchingly into our eyes when we blow it.

We must receive God's discipline for it to bear fruit in our lives. Hebrews 12:11 tells us, "No discipline seems pleasant at the time, but painful. Later on, however, it produces a harvest of righteousness and peace for those who have been trained by it."

I still laugh when I remember how my brother, Jimmy, used to run from my mother when she wanted to spank him. She'd chase him from room to room with her hairbrush while he cried, "How many? How many?" Of course, the longer it took for her to catch him, the more spankings he got.

This picture is funny but makes a serious point. If we won't allow God to "catch" us, how will we ever reap a "harvest of righteousness"?

4. God's discipline is tailored to each of us. God's discipline isn't handed out randomly. Just as I discipline Noah and Nathan differently according to their varied needs and personalities, so does God.

A well-known evangelist believes that God's church has become slothful, sugar-coated, and immune to the conviction of the Holy Spirit. Another popular evangelist asserts that the church today is under attack from legalism. He thinks we need more grace.

These two have theological differences. Who is right? They both are.

Some of God's children grew up undisciplined. They need a loving Father to look them in the eye and say, "Won't you stop sinning? It hurts me to see you hurt yourself."

Others of God's children grew up feeling naughty, as though they were never good enough. They constantly try to earn God's favor. They need to hear *Abba* Father say, "Hey, you're doing great. Relax and let me love you. Get to know my mercy."

We can't fully understand God's discipline until we know more about his love.

Abba Father's Love

"God is love" (1 Jn 4:16). However, intellectual knowledge doesn't convince the little girl inside who's been left or hurt by those who supposedly "loved" her.

Paul's prayer to the Ephesians is my prayer for you: "that you, being rooted and established in love, may have power, together with all the saints, to grasp how wide and long and high and deep is the love of Christ, and to know this love that surpasses knowledge—that you may be filled to the measure of all the fullness of God" (Eph 3:17-19).

Only God's love is powerful enough to fill in all the cracks and crevices father-loss left in our hearts. Here's why:

1. God's parental love is perfect. God's love is more than creator-object love. More than king-subject love. Perhaps above all it is parent-child love. "'I will be a Father to you, and you will be my sons and daughters, says the Lord Almighty'" (2 Cor 6:18).

John exclaimed in 1 John 3:1, "How great is the love the Father has lavished on us, that we should be called children of God! And that is what we are!" Are we as convinced of this as he was?

Several months ago, I was attending a week-long writer's conference with a girlfriend I hadn't seen for several years. We talked far into the night. I'd stayed up so late the previous two nights, I decided to take a nap. Then I realized with a stab of guilt that I hadn't spent any "quality" time with the Lord since I'd arrived. I'd spent all my time with people.

I climbed wearily onto my cot, ready to apologize to God. But then I heard him whisper to my heart, "Heather, you've got it all wrong! Remember? I'm your Father. I'm thrilled you're having such a wonderful time! I've delighted in watching you run here and there laughing and talking. I love to see you happy!"

I smiled in relief and closed my eyes. I imagined the Lord tucking the sheets under my chin. He wished me sweet dreams, anticipating a wonderful evening ahead for me and my friend.

Parents will go to great lengths—vacations, the zoo, the beach—just to see their kids laugh, smile, and have a good time. God loves us in that same way.

2. God's love is unconditional. The greatest difference between earthly parent-love and God's parent-love is that God's is unconditional. Maybe as a child you had to watch where you stepped around your father. You might have fallen through the thin, brittle floor of his collapsible love.

Standing on the unconditional love of *Abba* Father, we are free to run, jump, play, risk, and fail. God's love will never crumble or break beneath the weight of our mistakes.

Still, we struggle to believe this. We imagine that at any moment God will say, "Enough! I've had it with you—you'll never get it right!"

Father-loss is not the only factor that hinders our grasping God's Father-love. Satan is terrified at the thought of our becoming God's daughters. He wants us to believe that God is too mad to love us, that we are too unworthy. He wants us to close our hearts to God's love, for out of God's love we obey, and we love others. "We love because he first loved us" (1 Jn 4:19).

Revelation 12:10 describes Satan as "the accuser of our brothers, who accuses them before our God day and night."

What should you do when Satan nags and accuses you about your sin? Resist his lies about your worth. Then agree with him about the sin. "Yes, Satan, I shouldn't have done such and such. But guess what? My Father already knows about it—and he still loves me!"

Your Father does know already. And like a loving earthly father, he wants you to talk to him about it. Then he doesn't ever want to hear about it again—from anyone.

Can you see how God is your Father in the most down-to-earth, concrete way? He isn't a far-away God who makes you feel guilty all the time. He wants to relate to you in every area of life. He cares that your car died today, that your husband is mad at you, and that your son forgot about his soccer practice.

When you're angry at your mother, he wants to talk it over with you. When you're lonely, he wants to be with you. When you're weary of the world, feeling dirty and worthless, he is waiting. You're safe with him. At home.

Our Part: Becoming God's Daughters

God is faithful in love and discipline, the perfect Father. But unless we respond to him as his daughters, we won't understand his intent and devotion toward us.

I love Mark 10:13-16. "People were bringing little children to Jesus to have him touch them, but the disciples rebuked them. When Jesus saw this, he was indignant. He said to them, 'Let the little children come to me, and do not hinder them, for the kingdom of God belongs to such as these. I tell you the truth, anyone who will not receive the kingdom of God like a little child will never enter it.' And he took the children in his arms, put his hands on them and blessed them."

Many of you never had the opportunity to be little girls while you were growing up. You were forced to be good. You had to be strong in order to handle the trauma of a family sinking beneath icy waters. Now you must learn childlikeness. But how?

We learn much about how to be children with God by watching young kids in a healthy father-child relationship. Many of the ways they relate to a daddy are worth imitating in our relationship with *Abba* Father.

First, a little girl usually expects the best of Dad. Her daddy is Superman, Batman, and Mr. Rogers all wrapped up into one. To hear her brag about her dad to a playmate, one would think he was wonderful and strong and anything but ordinary.

Second, a young child wants to spend every available minute with her dad. Tagging along to the store is an event. Just to be with Dad is a good and wonderful thing.

Third, she is constantly displaying her affection for Dad. She wants to hold her daddy's hand, kiss him, and at times, climb all over him.

What kind of child are you with *Abba* Father? Do you brag about him to others? Sing his praises? How much time do you spend with him, not necessarily in deep prayer but just with him? And while you're with him, what is your posture? Do you bow down low before him in worship? Do you climb on his lap and let him lift your chin?

What do you call him? In Matthew 23:9 Jesus said, "And do not call anyone on earth 'father,' for you have one Father, and he is in heaven." God wants you to call him Father, Dad, and even Daddy.

The End of the Search

The first time my sister-in-law, Tami, left her toddler son for a few days, she phoned my brother to check on him after only a couple of hours. She heard Isaac crying hysterically in the background. Jim explained that Isaac had been running from room to room throughout the house looking for her.

Tami felt terrible. She wanted to pick him up and reassure him. She wanted him to know that she'd be back, that she'd never really leave him alone.

A physical barrier separates God from his children, one he longs to transcend. Tami said she could have died, it hurt so much to hear her son's pain. God did die. And still we doubt his love.

Are you like Isaac, running from room to room in life searching for your father? Stop and look up. You no longer have to ask, "Daddy, where were you?" Your Father has been there all along. Your search ends here in *Abba* Father's lap. You have found him forever.

The Beginning of a Future

Recently my mother sent me a photo of myself at about a year old. I hung it on my refrigerator door. Now and then I glance at it as I walk by—and I think of my father. Even as a baby, with my dark, wispy hair, I looked like him—and now that makes me glad.

If you remember, I opened this book by flipping through a

photo album and asking, "Daddy, where were you?" I don't ask that anymore. Today I know where both my fathers are. My earthly father is finally whole, the man God created him to be. Someday I'll see him like that, face to face.

It is hard to close this book, and I wonder what my tears are made of. Joy, made all the more real by pain. I know you understand. And I know that I'll see you someday—all of my sisters—on the lap of *Abba* Father.

Time to Consider

1. How has God begun to reveal his Father-love to you? What aspect of his love do you need most right now? His compassion? Forgiveness? Mercy? Guidance? Acceptance?

2. How do you think your relationship with God will change as you allow him to be your Father? What will make it easier to spend time with him? Will you laugh more or cry more? Will you allow him to take you into his den?

3. God is not only Father, he is Savior, Healer, Judge, King, and more. How do these aspects of his character work together and affect the kind of Father he is?

4. What is the next step for you to take toward *Abba* Father? Are you on his lap yet? If not, where are you? What is hindering you?

5. How can you help others discover their *Abba* Father?

Notes

ONE
Daddy, Where Were You?

1. David Blankenhorn, *Fatherless America* (New York, N.Y.: Basic Books, Harper Collins, 1995), 227, 235.
2. Regina McGlothlin, personal interview, Eugene, Ore., February 1990.
3. Marilee P. Dunker, *Days of Glory, Seasons of Night* (Grand Rapids, Mich.: Zondervan, 1984), 132–33.

TWO
I'll Do Anything

1. Elyce Wakerman, *Father-Loss* (Garden City, N.Y.: Doubleday, 1984), 18.
2. E. Mavis Hetherington, "Girls Without Fathers," *Psychology Today*, February 1973, 213.
3. Blankenhorn, 46.
4. David Popenoe, "A World Without Fathers," *The Wilson Quarterly*, Spring 1996.
5. Phame Camarena, quoted in *USA Today*, January 1993.
6. Wakerman, 213.

THREE
Won't You Be My Daddy?

1. Dunker, 133.
2. Regina McGlothlin, personal interview.
3. Josh McDowell, *His Image, My Image* (San Bernardino, Calif.: Here's Life, 1984), 81.
4. James Dobson, *Focus on the Family Bulletin*, June 1989.
5. McDowell, 81.

FOUR
Mother ... and the "Other"

1. Wakerman, 55.
2. Blankenhorn, 188.

FIVE
My Brother, My Sister

1. H. Norman Wright, *Always Daddy's Girl* (Ventura, Calif.: Regal, 1989), 170.

SIX
Who Am I?

1. Camarena, 6.
2. Deanna McClary, *Commitment to Love* (Nashville, Tenn.: Thomas Nelson, 1989), 34, 37.

SEVEN
It Still Hurts

1. McGlothlin, personal interview.
2. McGlothlin, personal interview.

EIGHT
Can I Cry Now?

1. Judy Tatelbaum, *The Courage to Grieve* (New York: Lippincott & Crowell, 1980), 66.
2. Natasha Tarpley, *Essence*, November 1994, 54.

NINE
I Want to Forgive, But ...

1. J.I. Packer, *Knowing God* (Downer's Grove, Ill.: InterVarsity Press, 1973), 125.
2. Rita Bennett, *Making Peace With the Inner Child of Your Past* (Old Tappan, N.J.: Revell, 1987), 159.

TEN
What Now, Dad?

1. James Dobson, *Emotions: Can You Trust Them?* (Ventura, Calif.: Regal, 1980), 98.
2. Wright, 218.